MY SISTER WAS
AN ONLY CHILD

ISBN 978-1-0881-2174-0

Manufactured in the United States

Distributed by Ingram

Hammonasset House
860.664.8028
HammonassetHouse.com
leejacobus@aol.com
Clinton, Connecticut

MY SISTER WAS AN
ONLY CHILD

A story of an Irish-American family
in New Jersey
before and after the Great Depression

Lee A. Jacobus

Hammonasset House

Table of Contents

FOREWORD

This is the story of my Irish-American family from the period of the Great Depression to the Eisenhower years. The struggles of the family were marked by a string of calamities and opportunities that may seem unlikely, but they marked our experience and shaped us all:

- My grandfather's total disinheritance in 1900 plunged my father and his brothers into poverty for most of his youth.
- The early death of my mother's father in 1913 sent her family into poverty when she was nine. The youngest of her three brothers was still in the womb.
- A special act of charity toward an ailing aunt unexpectedly helped the family buy the house on 7 Webster Place in 1930.
- My mother's dream gave my father the winning numbers he played on his way to work, saving the family home from foreclosure in 1933.
- My mother's youngest brother botched a bank robbery and found himself in the army in 1942.
- My father's rescuing an abandoned aunt with Alzheimer's disease proved one of the most painful experiences of the middle 1940s.
- My father's alcoholic brother broke in one

night and threatened us with murder.

- A daring Christmas Eve burglary while the family slept completely shocked our sense of security in 1948.

- With one grandmother in bed with cancer and the other grandmother in bed with a stroke, our house became a hospice until 1949.

- My beautiful sister suffered an unhappy childhood and, after jilting her wartime sweetheart, married the wrong man and made her life difficult and painful.

- White Flight in 1952 ended our years on Webster Place and began a series of moves that reduced the circumstances of my parents but gave them some security in their old age.

The story of my Irish-American family living in East Orange, New Jersey, covers a period of great political and social change. 7 Webster Place housed ten people in 1935 when I was born. I thought of myself as an only child, as did my older sister. We became aware of our conundrum only when we were much older and all the people of our youth were gone.

The Jazz Age: My Parents and How They Met

Every family, happy or not, has a story to tell about parents and how they shaped the lives of their children. Some parents are remembered for their absence, some for their presence, some for their limitations, some for their generosity. Some are remembered for their love, and some for their indifference. Some are remembered for their violence, some for their nurturance. Some, of course, are remembered because they inspired love in their children, and my parents were among those who gave much more to their family than their family could have given them back.

They were born into a perfect storm of poverty.

My grandfather, Ernest Jacobus, Sr., had been completely disowned by wealthy parents when he married Helena Brennan, an Irish Catholic girl who herself had come from a financially secure Irish family. My mother, Julia Rita Byrne, also from an originally comfortable Irish Catholic family, suffered the death of her father when she was nine years

Ernest and Julia in 1933,before they were married

old, forcing her mother to support four children with the work of her hands. My parents suffered extreme poverty in their childhood, and after marriage the residue of the Great Depression reduced them to a permanent condition of making do.

They were ordinary people dealing with extraordinary circumstances and enormous responsibilities early in their lives when other people were living a relatively easy – if not carefree – life appropriate to their age.

They were in their twenties during the "Jazz Age," but they did not remember much of the glamor and the excitement of that time. The New Orleans and Chicago style jazz I came to love was totally new to them. When at fourteen I mentioned King Oliver, Bubber Miley, Louis Armstrong, Chick Webb and other bandleaders of the time, they said that they had never heard their names or their tunes.

They were both products of not just the Roman Catholic Church, but the educational system of the Church. My father was born in 1903 and my mother in 1904. A Dutch Reformed Protestant, my grandfather converted and married my grandmother, an Irish Catholic, and was totally disowned by his wealthy parents and brothers. He became instantly not just a pariah, but a penniless nineteen year-old with no prospects. As a result of this, I never came to know anything about his extensive family. None of his family, brothers, uncles, cousins, ever contacted our family because of the curse–as far as they were concerned–of marrying an Irish Catholic.

My father, Ernest, Jr., a middle child, had four brothers close in age and his stories of family life were filled with hardships that seemed to me to be almost impossible to believe. There was no heat in any bedroom in the northern New Jersey winters, no money to buy extra winter clothes. The brothers crowded in one large bed. Ernest Sr. worked in Thomas Edison's factory in West Orange, New Jersey, and personally repaired all the shoes in the family. My father and his brothers lined their shirts with newspaper as a shield against the cutting winds. One happy memory my father had was of the entire family pulling taffy in the kitchen, a treat that his father and mother could barely afford, and then not often.

My father worked in a bakery when he was nine, and, when only a few years older, in a printing plant that gilded Campbell's Soup labels, leaving him with gold ink plastering his cheeks and hair. He never went beyond the eighth grade despite the fact that he was the best speller in his grade and clearly bright beyond his years.

His Protestant name made him the butt of the larger Catholic boys, who sometimes beat him mercilessly. They made fun of him because of his worn clothing and his general impoverishment. The children of the elite and privileged Catholic families were given preferment by the nuns and priests at St. John's School in Orange, New Jersey, while he was shunted to the back of the room. Once, he said, he had clearly out-spelled the children of the privileged in a school-wide contest, but the priest who officiated worked things out in such a way as to deny him his victory. Countenanced brutality and unfairness soured him on the church throughout his life. He almost never accompanied my mother and me on Sundays to Our Lady Help of Christians, our parish church on Main Street in East Orange. Despite her very strong argument and deep concerns, he went against my mother's wishes for me to go to

Catholic school. Indeed, he discouraged me from any social association with the church because of his own memories.

Julia, my mother, was, by contrast, totally devoted to the church, despite its not always being devoted to her. If anyone needed the help of the church, it was she and her family. Her mother, Margaret Hughes Byrne, lost her husband, Edward Byrne, a thirty-something steamfitter, to a bout of drinking and a fall in the snow that ultimately produced pneumonia and left her pregnant with her fourth child. My mother, nine when her father died, looked after her two brothers, Robert and Bill, and then in a few months, her infant brother, Edward.

Margaret Hughes had come from a successful Irish family in Bloomfield, New Jersey, and had prospects, but before she married found her way to the church convent and devoted herself to the nuns. Her enthusiasm, as I was later told, waned in proportion to the increasing venom of a belligerent nun who took special pleasure in demanding that Margaret get on her knees and scrub the gray cold stone floors in the anterooms of the nunnery. Such labor did not seem to her to be designed to glorify God, and Margaret left soon enough and was wooed by the handsome, swaggering strong-man who enjoyed ceilis, Irish dances, and feis, Irish games. Edward was said, by Margaret's brother, to have died holding the local record for throwing the hundred pound weight, an event that has long been discontinued as part of the feis.

Margaret lived partly on the charity of relatives, but primarily on the typical Irish labor of her own hands. She became a washerwoman and took in the laundry of the tenements in her neighborhood, using my mother as a delivery girl and helper. Her sons were much too young to help the family when it needed help most, but they must have had to find some work to increase the family income. Margaret lived with us when I was a child, and for many years I never understood why she was such a difficult and unhappy woman. Her life had been limited mercilessly, with no prospect of a change for the better.

The Byrnes were never homeless, but they never had enough. Yet, with all the struggling just to survive through the difficult years of the first world war, and the early 1920s, my mother somehow went to Catholic school in Bloomfield and learned to read and write very well, with especially beautiful handwriting. She was a lifelong reader, primarily of historical romances such as *Gone With the Wind*, and *A Tree Grows in Brooklyn*, her two favorite novels. Her love of reading contributed to her skills with language and made her career as a secretary quite logical. She practiced shorthand throughout her life, filling narrow lined notebooks with marks that meant nothing to me. In time she became adept at taking dictation.

With three difficult and demanding brothers, it is no surprise that Julia, my mother, left home as soon as she could. Her first marriage, at age eighteen to Thomas Westlake, was to a man I never met and whose photograph I never saw. Given her circumstances, my mother showed astonishing courage by divorcing him within a year or two of my sister Doris's birth in 1923. Her decision, and her follow-through, went against everything that her mother stood for. And not only did she stand up to her mother, but she accepted the greatest pain of all, the loss of the sacraments of the Church. As far as the Church was concerned, there was no such thing as divorce – except, of course, if the divorced were patrician, moneyed, and among the elite of the congregation. Then the problem could be solved in any one of a number of ways. For an ordinary woman like Julia, there was no hope of the Church's relenting. Charity was apparently a one way street.

Her decision obviously affected the rest of her life, but it also affected the life of my sister, Doris Westlake, into her late years. Doris never forgave my mother for her divorce – even years later, after Doris went through her own very painful divorce. My mother at first gave Doris over to the care of her paternal grandmother for a few years, and then later Margaret, our grandmother, looked after her when my mother moved back with her family and took over the job of supporting them all. Doris always felt that my mother had abandoned her when she was young, and because her father ignored her almost totally, she was emotionally damaged enough never to forgive what happened in her early childhood. The damage was lifelong, and nothing I could say to Doris, even when we were both full adults could ever make her feel better. She kept a relationship with our mother throughout life, but it was often grudging, and often based on Doris's venting her anger and disappointments for hours at a time over the telephone. My father, meanwhile, loved her and did all he could to help her through some very difficult times.

Another painful fact is that as a child, I knew nothing of my mother's early marriage, and it was only when I was thirteen or so that I began to ask questions that I knew I really should not be asking. Living in a strict Catholic family at that time did not encourage raising any emotional dust that might result from an unsettling inquiry. But one day I realized that my parents were approaching an anniversary that made it impossible for my sister to have been part of their family. My parents were married in 1933, when Doris was ten years old, and in 1946, Doris was married with one child, when I was eleven years old. The numbers did not work out the way I thought they should, so I asked my grandmother Margaret, who lived with us from 1940 until she died in 1949, how this disjunction could be accounted for.

Margaret was much more direct than my mother, but when she told me that my mother had been married before she married my father, and that Doris was my half-sister, I was sworn to absolute silence on the matter. My mother simply did not want me or anyone outside the family to know anything about her early marriage. And the truth was that she did not want to face the facts of her own youth. My father never mentioned anything about her first marriage at any time in my memory. Partly as a way of preserving the fiction of a single marriage, Julia lied about her age throughout her life. She lied so long that she was able to work into her seventies and when she applied to get her Social Security, she was awarded seven years back "pay" in order to bring her account up to date.

When I was very young my mother worked as a secretary in the front offices of Trommer's Brewery in Orange, New Jersey, a huge spread of redbrick buildings that, to my eyes, looked worn and strange. They formed a small campus with entries for large trucks that filled a parade ground where they loaded and unloaded racks of bottles and dented kegs that I could hear rolling across the cobbled stone alleys. The air was filled with an unusually powerful aroma of beer, It was a highly exotic place in my youthful experience because the street we lived on, while only a few blocks away, was a place of remove with small homes and only one relatively small apartment house,

Trommer's Brewery was in the middle of an African-American neighborhood where even as a young child I felt uncomfortable. I have no idea why I felt uncomfortable, although I realize that in 1941 or 1942 there was a race-riot in Orange right at the foot of our own street – an eighth of a mile from where we lived – that not only involved gunfire and terrible violence, but also arson and the destruction of many homes and businesses. Trommer's suffered only minor damage, but that catastrophe impressed itself on me when I was a child.

When I was only five or six, shortly before the race riots, I was sometimes in the care of a black woman named Mattie Adams. Mattie was probably in her fifties, large, sweet and caring, and she always wore a flowered housedress, much like those my grandmother wore. I remember loving her and wanting to be with her so much that one afternoon when she was leaving our house at the end of her day I suddenly volunteered to walk her home. It seems unlikely in some ways now, because I was so young, but Mattie lived only three blocks from our house, so I set off holding her hand, listening to the slap of her slipper-sandals, talking all the while until I left her off at her door. She told me to get on home now, and I stopped in front of a small gospel church on my way and heard the congregation's choir practicing. I have never forgotten listening to that extraordinary music, which sounded almost as loud on the street as it must have been inside. It was soaring and punctuated by hand claps and foot stomping and a kind of religious enthusiasm that was totally unknown to me. I stood there and stared through the open door and felt emotions I would never encounter again until decades passed. I remember walking home knowing I had heard something astonishing and unlike anything in my own church.

*

I have no idea how I learned that my parents met each other on a blind date set up by Betty Bush, one of my mother's married friends. Julia and Ernest were, on the surface, an unlikely couple. My mother, a secretary, had never stirred far from home. She did not quite live a sheltered life, but by no means was she a widely experienced woman. She was living with her mother and her daughter in straitened circumstances, but she was also able to go out with friends and enjoy something of life. By the time they met, my mother was fairly sophisticated, although at that time she did not smoke or go out drinking with friends.

Like most of her family, she went to church on Sundays and participated in most church holidays, paying special attention to Easter and Christmas, but also enjoying New Years Day and Thanksgiving. Things may have been hardscrabble, but however difficult, the priests and the church were central to my mother's life. But that being said, her early divorce made it emotionally and–according to church law–impossible to be absolutely one with the congregation. She could not take the sacrament of confession or communion, and that burden was with her for most of her life–until the church seemed to recognize modern reality and brought her, in her late 70s, back into the fold. I am not entirely sure how welcome she felt, or how much difference it made in her life. But in their 30s, she and Ernest were a bit of outsiders to the church, and that may have been an attraction for each of them.

Ernest and Judy in 1951

In his twenties, before he married, my father traveled all through New England and as far west as Chicago selling silver settings, silver trays, silver goblets, and silver services. He stayed at all the best hotels in Boston, Worcester, Cleveland, and New York. He described seeing Chicago gangsters speeding by in long dark sedans with their Tommy guns blazing. He visited every important speakeasy in the major cities, and he enjoyed himself. He traveled for the McChesney Company, then Black, Starr, and Gorham, and a number of other once well known makers of sterling silver services.

When he arrived in Chicago he would send out word to all the retail jewelers that his wares stood on display in one of the exhibition rooms of the Palmer House. The merchants saw all the new patterns and the standard pieces available that year. He laid out black velvet runners and positioned each of the items to take advantage of the light, then wrote up their orders. He laid out a dozen different silver place settings, repoussé and plain, carved and molded, sterling and plate. The coffee services stood near the chocolate pots and the tea services. The bowls and serving pieces stood by themselves. Trays, compotes, ice buckets, gravy boats, and novelty items shared their own quarter. A successful salesman, he returned from his trips wearing a camel's hair coat, the *ne plus ultra* of the time, a fine suit and tie and snappy shoes and hat. A handsome man with a steady job, he had the money to dress like a swell during the late twenties, with something of the flair of George Raft.

Ernest Jacobus in his 20s

Mr. McChesney once arrived in town at the same time as my father and knew about Ernest's prodigious memory for numbers. He was skeptical, So he appeared just as my father set up his wares, then asked him if it was true that he knew the item number of everything the company manufactured. "Yes," he told him, "And the catalog number, too." Mr. McChesney went up and down the rows, picking up each item and asking him to tell him the numbers. He did. Every one.

My mother must have been taken by his flair, and he was clearly taken with her own self confidence, built from years of surviving on her abilities and her skill at making it on her own. What he saw in her was a woman with a very powerful sense of herself, a strong will and a capacity to dominate those who were less quick witted and less confident. She was also a very fine looking woman with beautiful hair and expressive eyes. She had a flair for fashion and a marvelous way of moving through a room. By the time Ernest met her, she knew she was ready to have some fun in life.

My father's self-confidence, born of years of traveling alone and dealing with many kinds of people throughout his territories, matched hers, and in less than a year they began a marriage that lasted the rest of their lives.

Buying the Family House: Saving Aunt Mary

My childhood centered on our family house at 7 Webster Place in East Orange, New Jersey. The solid, unpretentious, one-family house at times contained up to ten of us. I took it for granted when I was eight years old, but later I wondered how my family came to own any house at all, given our essential poverty. My grandfather, Ernest Jacobus Sr., for example, worked in West Orange in Thomas Edison plants but never earned more than nine dollars a week. My grandmother Helena did not work, and none of her sons had jobs until my father went on the road as a salesman. His income was never large enough to buy or even maintain a single-family house.

The mystery unraveled one afternoon when my father told me a story about the early days. He grew eloquent describing difficulties the family overcame in order to stay afloat in hard times with five sons and Maria, an infant daughter lost to influenza. My grandfather and grandmother, Ernest Sr. and Helena, along with their children, originally rented tight quarters on High Street, Orange, in a tough neighborhood of Irish, Polish, Italian, and African-Americans struggling for survival. I saw it only once in a drive-by when I was about ten, a small house, grayish, indistinct, behind a low metal fence and a scruffy overgrown yard. A family crisis started the whole sequence of events that led to 7 Webster Place.

7 Webster Place: The family house in 1949

My father's Aunt Mary, Helena's much older sister, had grown infirm. She never married and had no children to care for her. In her youth, she was a strong-willed, energetic, and imaginative woman choosing a career over a husband, which made her an eccentric in the family. Working as a nutritionist for one of the local towns, serving the needs of the school system, she had a good salary and turned out to be remarkably entrepreneurial.

I was never told the nature of Aunt Mary's crisis, but it seems to have been a simple fact of aging and incompetence. She could not feed herself properly, a dangerous sign for a nutritionist. The house was unkempt. Aunt Mary, in her eighties, needed help. Our family took her in and fashioned a makeshift space. When my father sorted out her papers he discovered that Aunt Mary owned three small houses and had a large savings account.

On a cold but sunny day in the early 1930s Ernest Jr., Helena, and Aunt Mary all dressed in heavy coats got in a taxi and drove to her bank. They asked for the manager, and explained that they wished to close the account at that time. The manager ushered them into his inner office and discussed their plans. My father explained that Aunt Mary was giving up housekeeping and needed her savings in cash. Surprisingly, the manager acquiesced without a moment's hesitation. He had Aunt Mary sign a document closing the account, then went out to another room and came back with more than fifteen thousand dollars in cash in a stout brown envelope. He handed it to Aunt Mary, who during the interview said very little, and the three of them walked out and drove slowly down the main avenue of town back to their tenement on High Street.

Immediately afterward, my grandfather located the house at 7 Webster Place and took ownership. He moved the family in and placed Aunt Mary in one of the front bedrooms, taking the other front bedroom for himself and Helena. Ernest and his four brothers found their own spaces and made the house a home. It became a happy home for Aunt Mary, who improved in the company of people who loved her.

Aunt Mary had other relatives. None of them knew about the nest egg of cash she had preserved and none of them knew it had purchased a family home that would house and care for her until her death. I met some of the relatives in later years. They were Irish and roguish and still had a touch of the brogue on them. Most of them lived in Jersey City, which partly accounted for the intensely idiosyncratic pronunciation of most of their words. I remember playing football with one of them, Buddy, and finding him a very easygoing and pleasant fellow. He had the kind of charm that made it easy to cadge drinks and impossible to stay married.

His mother was also one of my father's aunts, Aunt Kitty, but I saw very little of her. She smoked cigarettes, cigars, and sometimes pipes. A haze of smoke always hung about her. She came to our house one Christmas Eve morning in an old "woody" Ford with the back of the car completely filled with stuffed animals and toys. A tennis racquet, the first I ever saw, stuck up in the back of her car next to a four foot long Christmas stocking, red mesh, filled with small toys. She played Santa Claus for the family with panache. Kitty, sharp-tongued and rough-hewn, married a man who sat around the house in his undershirt drinking beer. He never said more than two or three words. They lived in Asbury Park, on what we called the New Jersey Shore, in a neighborhood that was makeshift and less permanent appearing than any neighborhood we new in the Oranges, where we lived.

No one else in the family did anything to help Aunt Mary. Kitty, her much younger sister, was too busy and too far away. More distant members of the family, all those who lived in Jersey City, ignored her and did not visit her once while she lived at 7 Webster Place. My grandparents took care of her every day. They fed her, clothed her, kept her as cheerful as they could, and made sure she understood the importance of her role in the family.

Now, I cannot be sure what year Aunt Mary joined the

family, nor what year they actually purchased the house on Webster Place. My guess is that it was during the early years of the Depression, possibly 1931 or 1932. Aunt Mary died in October, 1938, after my third birthday. This detail is important because the first act of revenge I ever committed was against Aunt Mary.

I have no memory of what I did. On the other hand, I do have a dim memory of standing in a play pen in the dining room of 7 Webster Place. I recall seeing the light from the windows. I recall standing inside the playpen and I recall lying close to the floor: odd memories, disconnected, but palpable. I could not have been more than two and a half at that time.

As the first Jacobus grandchild, my grandparents made much of me as I puttered around in my pen. Aunt Mary had little else to do but keep track of me and she played a game that I didn't like. I had a head of long golden curls from age one and she enjoyed reaching down into my playpen and tugging at them. Strange that I do not remember a bit of this. But I often heard how Aunt Mary leaned into my play pen teasing me gently, but ending with a smart tug on my hair.

I put an end to that one day. She had been up to her tricks and kootchy-kooing at me until she got ready to reach down and pull my curls. When she did, I reached up and grabbed two handfuls of her hair, long gray hair, and would not let go. She yelled and straightened up, but I was attached and rose from the floor with her. It took the entire family to make me give up my victory. However I never had to deal with Aunt Mary's hair pulling again. She may have been senile, but she learned her lesson.

Probably typical of many families, when Aunt Mary

died, all the relatives on her side who had never come to visit, who had never written, who had never called to see how she was doing or find out what she needed, descended on the house on Webster Place to talk with Helena, my father's mother. The plans for the wake had gone off as they always had. The funeral was in my grandparents' local parish church, St. John's in Orange, and well attended. The proper words were spoken and the Brennan gravesite, with its tall winged angel and cross, was filled. And then the relatives came to see what Aunt Mary left to them.

They arrived in an agitated state. They knew enough to wait through the important mortuary ceremonies and to affect the appropriate mourning and sense of loss. But they worried about how much money she left them.

Despite being a good businesswoman, she died with no will. Her relatives came with demands. They wanted Aunt Mary's house. They knew she owned it. But they knew little more.

My father, age thirty-five, faced them on behalf of his mother. He told the relatives that Aunt Mary owned a house and presented them with the deed. He told them that she had expressly wished them to have the house. This announcement "took the wind out of their sails," as my father put it. They had brought with them a contentious antagonism, speaking all the while with a knife-edge Jersey City Irish brawling tongue as if threatening violence. My father's offer melted them into a manageable mob.

Then, my father shocked them with further news. He presented the deeds for the other two houses that Aunt Mary owned and rented out. They had no idea that she was a woman of such economic strength and foresight.

When they realized that they inherited three houses instead of one, and when they saw that Helena offered no contest for any of this property, they became sweetness and light. Instead of an argument, they enjoyed a large meal at the dining room table with me watching on from the playpen. They drank beer and whisky and sang some songs—the ones, they said, Aunt Mary would have liked. And they left. Happy, much enriched, and none the wiser about the way in which Aunt Mary figured in the purchase of 7 Webster Place.

A Numbers Game: Saving 7 Webster Place

After they married, my parents lived for a short time with my father's parents at 7 Webster Place. During the depression, the taxes had gone unpaid for several years and the grocer's bill had ballooned. My father, at that time, was no longer a traveling salesman, but was lucky enough to have a job working six days a week for Handy & Harman, a precious metals refiner in New York City, but now he was hardly able to make ends meet. Yet it was a time when one of the most remarkable of events of my father's life took place.

My father commuted to New York to his office near the Fulton Fish Market. In 1936 the back taxes on 7 Webster Place stood close to four hundred dollars and had not been paid in many years. Erhmann's Market had provided food to the family on a credit system and my grandfather owed some two hundred dollars.

Each day my father commuted to New York with only his fare money and his lunch money, fifty cents. He usually took a dime and played the numbers with a grocer on Fulton Street near work. The last three digits of the published daily shipping tonnage in New York Harbor posted in the New

York *Herald Tribune* business section determined the daily winning number.

One night before my father went to work my mother had a dream. She came close to not telling him about it, but she got up and cooked his breakfast and while he ate, she told him her dream: she was shopping for shoes in a fancy shop on Central Avenue, and whenever the clerk went for a box to pull down a new pair of shoes it always had the same number on it. Two hundred one. My father listened but he dismissed it at first because he had a method based on daily observation. Dreams didn't usually figure into it.

At seven a.m. when he walked over to Brick Church Plaza for the Lackawanna train into Hoboken, he stood still on the platform until the train stopped. The new coach in front of him was number two hundred one. The ferry in Hoboken pulled in with the number two hundred one prominent on the wheelhouse. When he reached Fulton Street a bakery van backed up right in front of him, almost running him over. Number two hundred one. That convinced him. He had no lunch that day, but put his entire fifty cents on two hundred one to win. And it won.

Amazingly, he found out the next morning that he won more than eight hundred dollars, a fortune at that time. He took the money home, paid off the·back taxes and saved the house. Then he went down the street and counted out the money he owed to Erhmann's Market, and in that one stroke my father put the finances back on an even keel and saved the family home. We talked about that miracle many times over the years and every time it was clear that the meaning of that moment was indelibly writ. For my parents it seemed a form of divine intervention.

I realize now that some of the money they won must have been the down payment on the house across the street, 22 Webster Place, that my father and mother bought as their own. Moving there in 1938 made it possible for my grandmother Margaret and my sister Doris to live with us.

22 Webster Place, my parents' first home,
across the street from my grandparents.

My grandmother had a large room of her own on the first level, while my sister Doris had the third floor, a spacious apartment where I used to visit and dance with her early in the morning to programs like the Milkman's Matinee on WNEW. The first floor was also where I slept, while the second floor was usually let out to roomers, some of whom followed us when we moved. For a time Bill Byrne, one of my cousins, stayed with us as well. It is clear now – although I was unaware of the reasons at the time – that my parents were not able to maintain the house without the extra rent from our roomers.

We had many roomers who stayed for a short time and some who stayed for at least a year or more. One young couple had a beautiful full grown Airedale dog who loped up and down the stairs like a puppy. His "parents" were a bit elegant and raffish in their manner and dress, and while they were polite and very cheerful all the time, they spent only a little time talking to me. I was very young and eager to talk, while they always seemed busy. A long term roomer was Mrs. Pearson, a middle-aged woman who worked in East Orange and always dressed very formally. She dressed like a saleswoman or executive in Bamberger's department store or in Peck and Peck. Unlike the young couple with the dog, she spoke with me often and seemed to enjoy my attentiveness. She was the first person to explain astrological signs to me. She took astrology very seriously and described my sign, Leo, and its importance. She even told my fortune out on the porch of the yellow house at 22 Webster Place. Amazingly, she told me I was destined to be a teacher, a prophecy I resisted for many years.

Our roomer in the marvelous large front room upstairs, the one with the oversized bowed window, was a Mr. Schmidt. He was German, spoke very softly and with a slight accent, and kept very much to himself. My father found him interesting, but he rarely spoke with him except to get his rent, and often Mr. Schmidt would leave his rent money in the kitchen when no one was there to see him. He was neat, polite, and rarely home. We were shocked when one Saturday morning in early 1942 government agents came to the house and asked when was the last time we saw Mr. Schmidt. My father told them it had been several days and we were worried about him. The agents explained that they were intending to arrest him as a

German agent. They would tell us nothing more. They went up to search his room, but found very little. Mr. Schmidt had apparently cleaned everything out without our knowing it.

However, he did not take everything. I went into the room and saw that he had left some books, none of which interested me. There was a large walk-in closet in the room in which he had a small box with a few coins, some collar studs, and a pocket-sized red leather book in which he had some writing in German. The agents had apparently seen it and disregarded it, but I found it interesting primarily because I had not seen another language in script. In the back of the book were some symbols that I realized were code symbols. I had just read Edgar Allan Poe's "Gold Bug" and was excited by the prospect of using a code to make my notes to myself totally private. Mr. Schmidt's book did not have any coded messages, just some Egyptian hieroglyphics and unusual letters that I decided to use as the basis of my own code. I kept that book for many years until I lost it in one of our many moves.

While we lived across the street from my grandparents, my grandfather kept the roof over his sons' heads while several of them could not find work. My father's older brother Jack had a good job, and his family lived for a short time at 7 Webster Place with his brothers and parents, as our family had done. Jack was a tall, dashing man whose fame spread to New York City, where he and his brother Richard won silver cups for their ballroom dancing skills. My father reminded them that there was no silver in their "silver" cups, and he felt disdain because he thought winning prizes at dancing was no way to help the family survive.

My memories of 22 Webster Place, the yellow house

across the street from my grandparents, center on my sister, who seemed to me to be the most beautiful and glamorous girl I could imagine. She was tall and willowy, with lovely chestnut hair, and a sweet disposition. She worked after school in the local five and dime store behind the candy counter, where I visited her. She was let go, she said, because she could not resist sampling the merchandise. She was a student at the Catholic school at Our Lady Help of Christians church and was doing very well scholastically. My mother's ambition was for Doris to become a nurse – an achievement Doris eventually realized, but not until many years later when she was in her forties.

Doris had a boyfriend we called only by his last name, Mullen, whom I can still picture. He was a senior in high school, handsome, cheerful, and quite clearly in love with Doris. He and she would go out into our backyard for the chance to talk privately, and of course I would chase after them as any four or five year-old would. Instead of shooing me off, they sometimes included me. I still recall our lying in the grass looking up at the sky in the summer of 1940, and I remained radiantly happy with them.

Another happy memory was visiting my grandparents on Sundays and having the traditional family meal in their large yellow kitchen. My grandfather sat me on his knee while I watched him fill and light his pipe. He had a large rocking chair off the rarely used dining room, and I could always count on seeing him there on Sundays.

My grandfather worked for Thomas Edison in the factory on Main Street. In my youth I found it ramshackle, with cobbled roadways, empty sheds, rusted ironwork, scattered machines, and worried looking men. My grandfather was a tool maker for Edison for twenty-five years or more. But when I was a child he had been laid off in his fifties. He had no pension, no health insurance, no social security, and no prospects. He was laid off with no more warning than a few rumor-filled weeks when everyone in the factory grew fearful for their jobs. Some of the younger men stayed on, but the older, slower workers were let go.

Sundays at the family home were always exciting for me. Everyone came back to the house after mass and the women in the family prepared the meal. Meanwhile, my uncles, Alfred, Paul, and Richard would sit on the cushioned chairs that ringed the dining room table and read the newspaper. But curiously they did not just read it, they sequestered parts of it. For example, Alfred would grab the Newark Evening News first, take the sports section and slide it under the cushion of his chair, then read one of the next most interesting sections, while Paul would take the comics pages and slide them under his cushion and read the styles sections. Richard would take the Star-Ledger and essentially do the same by sequestering a section he wanted to read later. It was a triumph for me to get the comics after Paul was finished with them. My father would call out and ask, "Who has the front page?" Some of the time he got an answer, but often all he heard was silence. I thought all this was the way everybody dealt with Sunday's papers.

A Grandfather Disowned and Scorned

I retain fond memories of the only grandfather I knew, my father's father, Ernest Sr. Like Helena, gentle, kind, and even-tempered, he never raised his voice in anger and he chastised me only once, when I played with a metal toy car on an enameled meat showcase at Erhmann's Market. He simply asked me, at the request of Mr. Erhmann, to stop running my car along the beveled edge that seemed such a perfect track for me. That I remember such a gentle reproof tells me how unusual it was. I could not have been more than four years old. Although I knew him for only a short time (he died when I was five), I had a great feeling of love for him. His quiet personality was firmly in place. This may be an odd thing to say, but I mean it just as it sounds. I felt his presence strongly and when we talked we truly achieved a meeting of minds. Perhaps he just loved children, and perhaps he just loved having a grandson.

When I was four we lived across the street. After having

Ernest Wilson Jacobus, my grandfather, in 1935
holding me next to 7 Webster Place.

lived with his parents for a year or so, my father somehow bought a house just a short distance away. I assume he used some of his numbers winnings. But however he did it, I know that my mother was overjoyed to have a space of her own, even though she had to share some of it with roomers. On Webster Place most of our neighbors rented rooms. It was the Depression and everyone learned how to survive.

Our house was yellow and had no driveway. As a result, my father parked our car in my grandfather's back yard, which also meant that we came across the street to his house almost every day. This commerce comforted my father and my grandfather, and surely comforted me, but I wonder now how comfortable it was for my mother. I don't recall her complaining about it, but then she would have complained in private to my father, not to me.

As a child I knew nothing whatever of my grandfather's background or his growing up. All I knew was that he was sweet, gentle, and interesting. But he was different from the rest of the family. For one thing he was not Irish. He was Dutch and English and originally a member of a Holland church possibly in Caldwell, the seat of the family. Although he had little education himself, he came from an educated family and his people enjoyed position and substance. He had several wealthy brothers, none of whom I ever met or saw. I never met anyone from his family because they disowned him when he married.

His choices forced him into the life of a common laborer. Ironically, one of his father's brothers, owner of a construction company, built not only the home of the former president Grover Cleveland, but also the home in which my mother was born.

Such total family rejections seem medieval now, but in those days his parents, avid and cultivated Protestants, harbored great contempt for Catholics, particularly impoverished Irish Catholics. They warned him that he would inherit nothing should he marry, but he went ahead and married anyway. His entire family was well to do. Businesses in New Jersey still bear his last name. The family was also educated, with several members in possession of university degrees. Unfortunately, their educations did not extend their humanity toward my grandfather. At one point my grandfather's mother saw him alone pushing my father in a pram and when she saw my father as an infant she offered to take him, raise him as her own, and provide him with an education. Ernest Sr. was shocked and refused. His mother made the offer several times and he refused several times.

While his father had nothing more to do with him, his older brothers had a successful coffee importing business in New York City. One of them, in an apparent act of charity, offered him a clerk's job in the company. Ernest Sr. accepted probably because he had no other prospects. His relationship with his brothers was difficult. Certainly they sided with their parents in regarding his fall from grace as warranted by his bad judgment. But at least they gave him a chance.

The job did not last long. In the third week, he came into the office and opened his desk drawer to find a five-dollar bill. He picked it up and brought it into his eldest brother's office and told him that he'd found the bill and did not know who it belonged to or how it found its way into his desk. With that, his brother with a big smile on his face explained that he and his brothers had placed the bill there just to test him, to see whether he would keep it or not. Ernest Sr. left immediately, put on his cap and walked out never to return. All this was told to me many years later.

The eldest brother seems to have had a modicum of conscience, although expressed in very strange ways. According to my father, after Ernest Sr. bought 7 Webster Place, and earlier when he lived on White Street, his eldest brother stopped by each Christmas morning. It was the only contact Ernest Sr. had with his family after he left the coffee business. The visit became a ritual. After church, Ernest Sr.'s brother came to the door in his chauffeured Rolls Royce. He stepped out of the car in a fur coat and top hat and went up the steps of the porch to ring the bell. When Ernest Sr. came to the door, his brother gave him a fifty-cent piece, asked after his health, and then left without setting foot into the house. I never saw this happen, but it went on throughout the 1920s and ended in the early 1930s, when Ernest Sr.'s eldest brother lost most of his holdings in the Depression. I have no idea what happened to the rest of the family or whether any of them showed up at Ernest's funeral in March of 1941. But Ernest Sr. paid an astonishing price for the privilege of marrying the woman he loved.

My grandfather found work in Edison's main plant at the foot of the hill in West Orange. My grandfather worked his way up to become a tool maker for Edison, a skill he must have learned on the job. We still have several tools that he made out of scrap materials for his own use. One of them, an awl with a carefully shaped wood handle, is a particularly graceful and useful tool. From what I can tell, he worked for Edison for twenty-five years or more. But when I knew him he had long since been laid off.

When I was four and five years old, my grandfather had two jobs. One involved insurance policies. Ernest Sr. was not an insurance salesman, but he went to people's homes and collected the periodic fees they paid on insurance policies which, in those days, were a few dollars every three months. Ernest Sr. never learned to drive a car, but he owned a black, elegant secondhand La Salle. The La Salle for nineteen thirty-one was nothing more than the Cadillac of nineteen thirty with some trim and details altered. Ernest Sr. was somehow persuaded to purchase this car by his young son, my uncle Paul. Paul promised to drive Ernest Sr. to his clients so he could collect the fees, and some of the time he did so. But, in nineteen forty and nineteen forty-one he often took the car at the same time Ernest Sr. needed to make his rounds. As a result, my grandfather relied on an old bicycle with a metal clip on his trousers-leg. I saw him return in the early evening on the slow wobbly bicycle, very tired, his lunch pail hanging from the handlebars and the sweat showing through his white shirt.

Ernest Sr. usually wore white shirts, bow ties, and suspenders. His trousers were often dark and striped, and his shoes scuffed and brown. He smoked a pipe some of the time, but never while on his bicycle. In his last few years he also worked for a furniture company in Newark called Kirch's. In those days people bought furniture on a credit system that involved their paying fifty cents or a dollar a week. My grandfather went around on his bicycle collecting these pittances every day. I have no idea what he got paid, but it could not have been more than ten dollars a week. His earnings were nine dollars a week at Edison's.

I went with him on his rounds many times, but only when Paul drove the car and took him to his customers. Paul sometimes came out of the car and talked with the people, especially the young women. Otherwise, Paul would sit in the car and read the newspaper while my grandfather made his calls.

My grandfather had a very pleasant relationship with his customers. They greeted him by name and took a few minutes to hold a conversation with him. Very often they were out of doors when he came, so I must have been taken along in the warm summer months when I was four and five years old. I loved going on those trips. I had no idea what my grandfather did. For me it was a chance to get out and around, something uncommon in my childhood. It was also a chance to meet new people. They always treated me kindly and took time to kneel down and make me feel welcome and useful.

I still remember making a visit to one woman who lived in a nearby town in a house much like ours. She had a backyard with long, very dark green grass, quite different from our scrubby anemic side yard. It was like an ocean of thick hair on the ground. The woman knew my grandfather and greeted him kindly while she hung laundry from a long line in the backyard. She dropped a clothes pin and I ran gallantly over and picked it up to give to her. She was impressed with my courtesy and made a big point of thanking me. My grandfather valued courtesy and good behavior, and while I traveled with him I do not think I ever misbehaved.

There were a few difficult moments, however. The most difficult produced a moment of public embarrassment still etched in my memory. I was four years old in nineteen thirty-nine when my grandfather took me, along with some of the rest of the family, to the Hollywood Theater to see Charles Laughton in *The Hunchback of Notre Dame.* Everyone wanted to see this widely heralded movie. I was thrilled when I realized I was going with the family because it was my first experience in the cinema. The excitement and intensity of the film soon got to me. But when Quasimodo began swinging on the bellrope I came unglued. He was hideous, and threatening as he swung toward me and I screamed so loud that my grandfather carried me up the aisle while I hid my eyes. He walked me home and probably got me an ice cream to calm me down and he seemed to forgive me.

But I am sure he was disappointed to miss the film. I doubt he ever saw it again. On the other hand I realize now from that experience how profound an effect "literature" had on me at a tender age. My father told interesting stories about Ernest Sr. from his own childhood. On some Sundays Ernest made a supply of taffy for the children. The process involved taffy-pulling, but the results as described by my father seemed to be something more like a brittle. On different Sundays Ernest Sr. sat all the children down and cut their hair, using a convenient bowl.

Ernest Jr. (center) in need of a haircut wearing
the shirt his mother made for him.

My father appears in a photograph as a child after the bowl had
been used on him. Ernest Sr. also mended the children's shoes
using a variety of expedients. He patched holes with cardboard
and scraps of leather. Twine served for shoelaces and he
repaired split leather uppers where he could. In the winter time
he saved newspapers so the boys could put them layered under
their thin winter coats as protection against the wind. He was
an ingenious man working diligently to keep the family happy
and together.

My mother, on the other hand, reported that Ernest Sr.
often sat in the back bow-windowed room in a dark humor. In
these moods he would not speak to people. He simply sat and
stared. I never saw such behavior in him, but I believe it. Since
I bear some of the same genes, I recognize the signs of

depression and have done a bit of sitting and staring of my own. Given his life, he had a right to be depressed. He came from great comfort and promise and was thrust into lifelong deprivation and limitations of a sort he could never have imagined before he had to live with them.

Ernest Sr. died at age sixty-three. In the photograph I have of him holding me in 1935 he looks more like seventy-five than fifty-eight. He looks like my father and I am beginning to look like him myself. He died early on a March morning without warning from a massive heart attack. The men in the ambulance sat him on a chair and carried him down the front stairs from his bedroom and then down the stairs of the porch. They administered oxygen through a mask, but Ernest Sr. fought the mask away. It must have frightened him. He struggled all the way into the ambulance as if aware that it was his last ride. He died almost immediately upon arrival at the hospital.

I remember being dressed by my sister Doris. She put me in a new suit and was combing my dampened hair when the news came. We were upstairs on the third floor of 22 Webster Place near the front of the house and the low windows that looked down through the trees to the street. These were Doris' rooms. I broke out crying with an intensity that shocked people in the family. I had lost my grandfather and I loved my grandfather more than anybody. I didn't know what death was, but I knew it was final and that it meant I would not see my grandfather again, never visit his customers with him, and never walk down the street holding his hand again. It was more than I could bear at the time. I could not be brave, and I could not follow the directions I was given: to go outside and play.

The world was filled with too many important things for me to trivialize the moment by playing. I became a very serious five-year-old.

Aunt Emma, Uncle Paul's wife,
me, and Helena in 1942

The year 1941 brought a torrent of changes in our lives. With the declaration of war in December, 1941, things changed again. My uncle Paul was eligible for the draft the next year, and Doris' boyfriend, Mullen, who enlisted almost immediately, was away with his unit. While he was gone, another boy came along, Paul DiLeo, who had been in the marines in 1940, but who was released for medical reasons. He was a dashing fellow with a car, and he swept Doris off her feet. She dropped out of high school only a few months before graduation to get married, and in the process broke Mullen's heart, as well as mine. In addition, she broke my mother's heart. Julia had hoped Doris would be the first member of the family to graduate with a diploma from high school. Almost twenty years later, Doris got her GDE and then began college. Hers was a long haul.

My parents' financial situation changed suddenly with the loss of my mother's job at Trommer's Brewery. They were forced to sell the house across from 7 Webster Place only to move into a small apartment a few miles away, near my Nassau School, where I was in second grade. My grandmother Margaret moved along with us, but the apartment was very small and she was unhappy in a much tinier room in a neighborhood that had very few interesting places to explore. Her mood during that period was somewhat dark partly because she was enlisted to look after me while my mother found another job. That lasted less than a year until we could rent a house, also in East Orange, near the Sanford Street School at 45 Sanford Street. These moves were all driven by failing economics. My father was no longer traveling, but worked in an office for a very low salary, with no commissions, at Handy & Harman, where he stayed for thirty-seven years.

By 1944, things at 7 Webster Place became difficult. My uncle Alfred, the youngest, was declared unfit for the Armed Service, my uncle Richard, by a few years, was too old, and later my own father missed the draft by just a month. He was trained in first aid and fire prevention and given an arm band and a metal helmet so that he could be effective on the home front. He took his responsibilities very seriously throughout the war.

My uncle Richard, who like Alfred, still lived in the family house, wanted to move out because he was getting married. That would have left no one to care for my grandmother, Helena, now growing infirm in her late sixties. I say infirm, but the truth was that she had breast cancer in its early stages and would stay in bed for the next few years. No one ever told me that Helena had cancer because of the shame involved in mentioning the word. I learned what her illness was when my sister told me thirty years after the fact. Now, I marvel at the silence surrounding her circumstances just as I marvel at the absence of any medical treatment for her illness. I remember Helena having been visited often by priests, but never by a physician.

After a family consult, and in the face of Helena's illness, my father agreed to take the responsibility of the house and his mother and Alfred, who had no plans for leaving. But after we moved in, my father learned that his brother Richard had lent money to his father and now wanted it back so he could get married. The amount, $1500, was a fortune. It was $400 more than my father had paid for the yellow house across the street, and it became a difficult long-term burden for him to pay off.

But eventually my father paid Richard the money and the family house was ours. While we actually lived in it for only seven full years, 7 Webster Place remained for all of us the most important emotional center of our family life. No other house every represented the stability that we associated with home as that house did.

Aunt Jett: The Ravages of Alzheimer's Disease

Probably nothing more clearly defines my parents' generosity and their ability to survive through adversity than their decision to take in my Aunt Jeannette Brennan, my grandmother Helena's older sister. At that time–1946– in 7 Webster Place we already had the care of Helena, who at first was able to get up and down stairs, but was later bedridden for three years. In addition, both uncle Alfred Jacobus and my grandmother Margaret Byrne lived with us. Alfred, in his late thirties with no regular job, sometimes assisted his older brother Richard dressing windows in taverns and cigar stores in the neighborhood. Margaret did most of the cooking and cleaning, but she was never happy in the kitchen. Adding Aunt Jett to that mix was certainly too much to ask, but my father somehow convinced my reluctant mother to take her in. What neither of them knew was that Aunt Jett was suffering the early stages of Alzheimer's.

Jeanette Brennan, my father's aunt, lived most of her life in New York City at West 98th Street in a third floor walkup. I was ten when we visited her claustrophobic apartment. My father and I climbed a long set of dark stairs that wound back on themselves, ending on a landing with a smoke-darkened grated window near the door to her apartment. The walls were dark wood paneling typical of neighborhood tenements. A long hall opened into a narrow, dank kitchen where I felt the darkness and strange smells close in on me. Despite my sensing that this was an ominous moment I might have noticed much more about this visit if I had understood its importance to our lives. The three of us sat for several hours at the kitchen table. I traced designs in the frayed green and white oil cloth while my father asked Aunt Jett about her health, her visitors, her life. "Are things going all right for you? Do you need anything? Have you seen the Bennett boys and have the Finnerans been over to see you? How are you getting along?" My father's voice was low, steady, comforting. He touched her trembling hand once or twice and she smiled at him.

Aunt Jett just sat there faintly smiling most of the time. My father made her some tea. She stirred it with her spoon, smiling, but she said only a few words. She looked at me for a moment, asking about school. She seemed never to answer my father's questions directly. I was unaware that anything was odd, partly because I was used to being with quiet older people and was only as self-aware as most kids my age. I thought she was a nice woman, but I had no idea how she would affect our lives. My father learned that she had not seen anyone in the family for quite a long time and he knew right away that she was unfocused and distracted. He also thought she might have been ailing, even though she was not obviously ill.

What my father knew is that Jett had reached the point Aunt Mary had reached. At close to ninety years old, she could no longer take care of herself. Reflecting on it now, I cannot imagine how my father worked it out with my mother, who must have complained about having to take care of one more incapacitated relative. But on that day we brought Aunt Jett home to live with us. My father knew she could not manage her life alone any longer. She had very little food in the house when we visited her and did not seem to know how to get more. She had no money and no one to care for her. As a young woman she raised three of the Bennett boys all by herself. Buddy Bennett was in his thirties, away working. The other Bennett boys had long since disappeared. None of them could take care of her and my father insisted that someone who had spent much of her life caring for others in the family did not deserve to be abandoned. We brought her home and gave her the attic bedroom next to my uncle Alfred.

Although Aunt Jett lived with us for almost three years, our conversations never moved beyond trivialities, social niceties, and casual observations unaccountably abbreviated. I was confused by her, and sometimes not as patient with her as I should have been. Other people in the family spoke with me about serious matters and revealed some of their inner thoughts, but not Aunt Jett. She commented on things. Weather. Flowers. Odd pieces of furniture that sometimes seemed out of place. She liked the radiant sunlight streaming through the stained glass windows on the stairway landing. She was sweet and temperate in every way. But Aunt Jett remained essentially a mystery to me.

One thing I understood on a deep level was how good she was as a person. She never raised her voice, never complained, never demanded more or different than what she was given. Yet she had almost nothing to say. By contrast, I talked too much, and often all she would do is stare away with a slight smile on her face, or sometimes with little or no expression. Sometimes when she was first with us she smiled, chuckled, or responded in simple ways. I read some of the newspaper to her. But withal, I learned nothing about how Aunt Jett lived, what she had done in New York, or what she thought about the world around her. She praised my father for having been a good boy when he was young. She told me in bits and pieces how grateful she was to him for taking her in. She never talked about her own home, her other relatives, her life in New York City. She did not miss West 98th Street or much of anything else.

Despite her frail, slender appearance--about five foot three--she managed to go up and down several flights of stairs every day, always in a long black dress with a white frilled collar, much like the dress Helena wears in a photograph I have of her. I can still hear Aunt Jett's slippers clapping against the back kitchen stairs, slow, slightly erratic, persistent. My parents worried about her falling or breaking a bone, but she never did. When she wanted company they kept her special chair for her in the dining room. She sat in it and rocked for hours to a slow, rhythmic creaking as she stared ahead in silence. Although her life was profoundly circumscribed in those years, she had a family to interact with and to care for her needs.

When I was almost eleven years old I did something I knew I would regret. My friends were over at the house working on projects up in my room, the large middle room on the second floor. I was put up to it by an older playmate, a bully, but even though I knew better, I never resisted. We decided to play a prank on Aunt Jett. She was an eccentric in the neighborhood, a mystery to my friends, almost a ghost-like presence. We got some old clothes and stuffed them with pillows and towels to make a dummy almost my size. We tied a piece of clothesline to the dummy and waited for Aunt Jett to go down the main flight of stairs. The plan was to scare her.

We heard the attic door open and saw her close it gently behind her. Then she turned facing the stained glass windows at the foot of the first flight of stairs and grabbed hold of the bannister and walked steadily downward. When she reached the landing and studied the light through the stained glass windows, she turned to her left and began down the bottom flight of stairs. I then lifted the dummy over the bannisters on the top floor and just before she reached the bottom of the stairs let it fly, screaming, "Boo!"

It frightened the devil out of the poor woman. She lost her balance and fell against the paneling on her right, but she did not fall down the stairs or hurt herself. She shrieked and my mother ran to help her, saw the dummy and shouted up to me. She made damned sure I understood how bad this was. My friends still thought it a joke, but already I knew this was something I'd never forget. My mother disciplined me and kicked all my friends out of the house. I apologized to Aunt Jett and told her I was truly sorry. She seemed not to know what to make of it. I had the feeling that she thought I was the dummy myself.

*

Aunt Jett could not come to the movies with us. She walked too slowly, could not see very well, her hearing was dim, and she seemed content staying home. My parents only rarely went to the movies together, but there were times when they and I would want to walk to the Hollywood Theater on Central Avenue or the Palace Theater on Main Street. We had a serious problem, however, with leaving her alone in the house.

We would explain clearly that we were all going out. She seemed to understand. We would ask her to make herself comfortable in her room upstairs and to stay there until we returned. We wanted to avoid a fall or other emergency. I had to walk down to the corner of Webster Place and Harrison Street with my parents and then double back while they waited for me. I then snuck up the side of the house and peered in the kitchen window. When Aunt Jett came down stairs she always made her way to the gas stove, which sometimes had to be lighted with matches. Consequently, when she wanted to make herself some tea or a piece of toast by burning it over the gas she could never start the flame unless the pilot light was working. That spelled danger. We feared that the house would blow up some evening.

Our movie outings sometimes came to grief by my having to run inside, turn off the gas, and ask Aunt Jett to get out of the kitchen. I never said anything harsh to her, but I had to be firm. I would then run to the corner to tell my parents to come home. Our family outing would be postponed and Aunt Jett would disappear back up into her room.

Soon, Aunt Jett's problems became more serious. At night my father heard noises downstairs and found her distraught, trying to get breakfast ready in the dark at four a.m. He would turn on the light, make her some tea, sit down and talk quietly with her until she felt more calm and secure. Sometimes she became disoriented and agitated, and only my father could convince her that she could relax even though that dark impossible apartment on 98th Street no longer existed in her life. My father knew Aunt Jett was senile when he first rescued her, but he did not know how serious her condition could become. No one then had heard of Alzheimer's disease.

On evenings when she could not sleep she wandered through the house lost and fearful. My uncle Alfred, who slept in the room next to Aunt Jett's, reported that she went into his room and felt around in the dark, fingered his face and woke him in excited fear. Aunt Jett's behavior unnerved him much more than we thought reasonable. Alfred was jittery to begin with and Aunt Jett's midnight excursions made things all the more difficult for him.

With all of her difficulties there were a few comic moments early in her stay with us. Aunt Jett had almost no experience with automobiles. On the first Christmas only months after she came to live with us, my father transported her to a relative's house in our Model A Ford Roadster, a two-seater with a worn fabric top and a rumble seat, in which I rode. It was a typical snowy winter night when my father helped her out of the house and into the car. At that time she was quite able to walk on her own, but he helped her around the snow mounds, down the steps, and opened the passenger door for her. She began to get in and he thought she had things under control. While she fitted herself inside, he closed her door, turned and said goodnight to people.

As he opened the driver's side door, he heard Aunt Jett's muffled comment, "A grand car that you've got, but the ceiling is awfully low." He asked her what she meant and at the same time slid into the seat only to find that Aunt Jett did not have her feet on the floor. She had managed to climb up on the seat itself and perched her bottom on top of the seat back. This meant she had somehow doubled herself over under the roof of the car. Her back was against the roof and her forehead against the windshield. No wonder it seemed so low. My father did not laugh at the time, but for years after, whenever the conversation rolled around to Aunt Jett, he told this story.

After three difficult years, Aunt Jett becme a burden that my family could not manage. Helena was bedridden, Alfred in the hospital with life-threatening stomach problems, and Margaret was not well. Aunt Jett at ninety-three grew incompetent. She knew my father, but little more. My father, against everything he believed in, had to find an institutional place for her. My mother simply could not continue with the situation as it was. They knew only of Overbrook Hospital, the state facility in Caldwell, the home for the insane. In those days everyone knew about Overbrook, but no one spoke about it. It loomed as a threat in the lives of everyone, young and old.

The Wing for the Extremely Aged accepted her. Large, old maples and oaks shaded the grounds of the asylum. For many months my father and I got up early on Saturday morning and made the long drive out to visit Aunt Jett. At first, I went into the forbidding redbrick building with my father. In good weather we took her outside to a picnic table and tried to talk with her, but the conversation never changed. Aunt Jett pleaded with my father to take her back to Webster Place. She became like a child, insistent, frightened. Her voice quavered. Her hands trembled and clutched for my father. He could not take her home. He could hardly talk to her when she became so

Front View of Insane Asylum, Overbrook, N. J. ⟨handwritten text⟩

Overbrook Hospital for the Insane

intense. On our ride home my father would sometimes be in tears and I had no way of helping him through his grief.

In cold weather we went indoors and sat with her at a refectory table made of slabs of oak, with ridges deep from scrubbing. The crevasses between the wood held deposits of food, grease, and an institutional green soap. Aunt Jett ended her pleading to come home. I knew she could not come home, and while I felt moved by her pleas they did not affect me in the way they affected my father. He knew how she had cared for her own family members. He knew legends about her youth. For example, one story about Aunt Jett that was always mentioned is that she was blessed as an infant by sitting in the lap of Abraham Lincoln. I was told that he stopped in a train while campaigning in New Jersey and that Aunt Jett's mother held her up for the president to see and Lincoln cradled her for a short while and handed her back. Such tales may be apocryphal, but my father had known her as a woman in the fullness of life. I had known only a shadow of that woman.

In a few months I could no longer go in with my father to see Aunt Jett. It was too painful for me. Their visit became little more than silent vigils. My father talked, mentioned some relatives, passed on some news, and searched for her reactions. She had no reactions. She essentially shut down. I stayed out in the car.

I read *Popular Mechanics* and *Popular Science*. I sat alone poring over the classified ads in the back of the magazines, and I read every article straight through. I marveled at the cars of the future, the space stations that would circle the earth with colonies of fortunate tourists, and the energy revolutions that loomed only years away. Outside the car windows I watched inmates wander the lawns like shades. They stopped near the car, leaned toward my window and stared at me. Women constantly screamed behind the walls. We always parked the car next to the redbrick building of the aged women's wing. From behind the windows came the wailing of abandoned women crying into their rooms and out their windows. It was terrifying and I have never heard anything like it since.

Finally I found excuses not to go with my father on those gloomy trips. Now I regret that I let him go it alone. By then Aunt Jett did not recognize him at all. She sat slumped and tiny in a gray uniform, her eyes sunken, her hair thin wisps of gray straggles, her large ears pale, her lips quivering. Yet he never stopped visiting her. Every Saturday. An hour's drive. An act of devotion until the end.

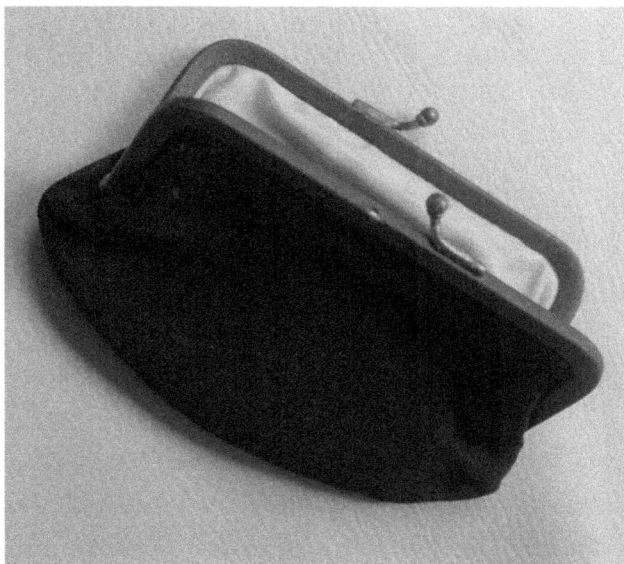

Aunt Jett's purse

When my father died, some forty years after our visit to West 98th Street and more than thirty-five years after Aunt Jett died, I found an old manilla envelope with some materials he saved from those days. In it a worn black woman's change purse contained ninety-three cents and a piece of paper with a note in my father's hand: "All the money Jett had when she came to live with us." Except for the clothes on her back, that purse was the only thing she brought with her to Webster Place.

My Mother's Joy: Judy's Silver Shop

My mother was thirty-one and her hair was chestnut brown when I was born, but I remember her hair only as white. I falsely imagined her hair had turned white after an automobile accident that was a defining moment in her life, but that took place in the 1920s when she was riding with some friends in the back of a two-door car. She was a nervous passenger of the "Look out!" variety and the "Be careful!" sort. Late one night, driving with three other young women, a truck bore down on them and seemed certain to hit them. My mother panicked, pushed the driver's seat forward, got the door open and put a leg out just as the truck hit the car. The driver of her car was hurt as the pushed-forward seat pinned her to the steering wheel. My mother's shin bone was snapped in two and she suffered astonishing pain.

At that time doctors lined the bones up, put them in a cast, and ordered bed rest, which for Judy lasted more than

Julia Byrne in the mid 1920s

a year. My sister lived part of that time in Belleville with her paternal grandmother and my mother lived with her mother in an upstairs bedroom. My mother's terror on the highway led to the crash, which might not have happened if she hadn't made it impossible for the driver of her car to get out of the way of the truck. But that's guesswork. The reality is that she lived with pain and uncertainty in her leg for the rest of her life. She had a small oval-shaped wound on her right shin which always had a scab, or what appeared to be a scab. We always had to be careful of that leg, and as a child I was warned not to bring heavy toys or balls near it. Her fear was that it would break again, which, given the nature of broken tibias, was an all too real possibility.

The outcome of the accident included an insurance settlement of several thousand dollars. One of my mother's distant relatives by marriage, Dick Spitz, a lawyer in Newark, helped her sue the insurance company. It took years for a settlement to come forward, but eventually my mother got enough money for new furniture. She bought a sofa and side chairs and a bedroom suite in the art deco style that remained with her throughout her life. These physical objects were held in some reverence in the household not because of their intrinsic value, but because of the pain that had gone into their purchase.

Another extraordinary shock occurred when she was a child. I was thirteen before I noticed that my mother had a strange indentation in the skin directly in the middle of her right forearm. Her long sleeves usually covered that spot. But when I asked her about it she amazed me by explaining that she had been shot accidentally by Robby, one of her younger brothers. She was coming down the stairs while he aimed his father's naval revolver at her in play. When he shot she had her arm up toward her face and the bullet went between the bones of her forearm, lodging in the wall above her. As a result, she never wanted to have guns anywhere near her and was anxious always to have my grandfather Ernest's pistol removed from the hall closet .

Another event from her childhood seems almost surreal, something one might expect from an early French film. She recalls having been on her front stoop in White Street where they lived in a row of identical tenements. Each stoop was separated from the other by a waist high fence with white bannisters. As a little girl she suddenly heard and saw a milkman's horse racing from stoop to stoop, jumping each fence one after the other and she threw herself on the floor next to the bannisters on her stoop and began crying. The horse leaped over without touching her and continued until it reached the street where its owner, running after him on the sidewalk, shouted for the horse to stop. The milkman's nag also jumped over a baby in its carriage along the way, averting certain disaster. Among the few things that my mother told me about her childhood, she often repeated this story.

In the 1940s my mother had several jobs, but her most interesting and pleasing work began when I was close to twelve. In 1946 my father had many contacts in the jewelry trade in New York. He suggested they start a shop to sell silver handmade jewelry and my mother was thrilled at the thought. They found a vacant shop nearby in Brick Church Plaza, East Orange, in the shadow of my father's train. It was a small shop on the corner, set back from the road, a stucco building with a low roof designed to look vaguely Dickensian with a suggestion of the Cotswold region. My mother's new stationery used Old English typeface to keep in the spirit. The Plaza had ten shops in a row, more or less alike, not all the same size, but all cozy and charming. My mother's was about sixteen by fourteen feet in size, with a small bathroom and a closet. The two show windows were slanted panels covered with black velvet and with a low curtain to give a little privacy to the interior of the shop.

Julia must have been happier while she had the shop than at any other time of her life. Partly because she had been an experienced and competent secretary for several men in different lines of business, she excelled at all the phases of shop keeping. She kept the books immaculately. She kept track of all the hand-made pieces of silver that were brought from the makers in New York, and she had an excellent eye for what would sell and what would languish. Beyond that, she had a fine manner with people who came in to browse. She had a good supply of small talk and conversation and learned all she needed to know about the jewelry she had to sell. I visited her regularly on my way home from school and often sat with her for a half-hour or longer before continuing on home to Webster Place.

Those were happy times. Her conversation was bright, as was her expression, and she was filled with a special kind of seriousness and joy. She ran her own show and had a marvelous time doing it. While I visited, she always worked with some piece of jewelry or talked with a customer or dealt with the bookkeeping. She named it *Judy's Silver Shop* and it became well known in East Orange.

She sold high quality items, both in terms of the intrinsic value and in terms of the artistic level of the work. Her extensive stock was sterling silver jewelry, pins, rings, ear rings, brooches, cups, bowls, and vases, but no place settings. All her merchandise was hand made by my father's customers. He found the goods, my mother vetted each piece, tagged it, recorded it, and then sold it. At the time, however, I had no sense that the earnings from the shop were any greater than the earnings she had from working as a secretary. The shop did not produce much money, but it did make my mother feel important and independent.

Fortunately the shop was never robbed. My parents never appeared worried about burglary, and as far as I know, none of the stores in the Plaza was ever struck. There was a small nightclub called *The Normandy* down some seven or eight shops away, and once there was an major altercation of some kind there. But it never disturbed my mother or her ambitions to make her shop a destination for people interested in unusual jewelry. Just to be sure, however, a large sturdy safe stood in an alcove to protect her inventory. My mother removed everything from the window each evening and put it in the safe until the morning. One of her pleasures each day was making the window look inviting. She was good at that too. She had an accomplished eye for good design.

These were years when my grandmother Margaret Byrne was able to look after the house. She was not always happy to do so, but by and large she was able to keep everything working as it should. Aunt Jett was in Overbrook, which meant that my mother was not needed to look after her or to worry about Aunt Jett's wanderings or her needs. My uncle Alfred was still in the house, but by this time he had found some work in The Big Bear, a grocery that eventually made it possible for him to find his own apartment. He worked in that grocery chain for the rest of his working life and his pension supported him until death.

My grandmother Helena was by this time bed-ridden. She was in the last phases of breast cancer, and spent almost three years in bed before the cancer killed her. These were difficult times, but they were only the beginning. I was able to take up some of the tasks of caring for Helena by bringing her meals to her, by spending some time with her while she was able to converse. Like Aunt Jett, my grandmother Helena was not a conversationalist. We did talk, but I am sure now that it was I doing most of the talking. Helena had questions, and was always after me to tell her about what I was doing in school and elsewhere, but she never said anything about her own experiences as a child or as a young woman. Today that puzzles me, because I am full of questions that I would like to have answered. For instance, I would like to know what Helena's parents were like, or even who they were. They were never mentioned in our household. I knew the family name, Brennan, but beyond that I knew nothing. I did not know what her early life with Ernest Sr., my grandfather, was like, nor after he died did I know much of anything about her own feelings or her hopes. She may have been depressed, but in those days the idea of depression was not as common as it is today.

The only hint of depression that I knew about came from my sister Doris, who in her few years living with the family in 7 Webster Place and across the street in 22 Webster Place felt that my grandfather Ernest Sr. was very dark in his moods. I could not have detected that. But when I reflect on how his life was limited by lack of opportunity, and when I put that together with what I knew about my father's character and intelligence, I can easily see why he may have felt a sense of almost total desperation. Ernest Sr. must have been aware of the terrible loss to himself of the chance to go to college, like his brothers, or to pursue a profession – all a result of his having married my grandmother. People possessed with talent and intelligence, and thus aware of their being denied the opportunity to put their talents to the test, must share a similar sense of injustice and regret. If he suffered dark moods caused by his limitations and his inability to earn more than the minimum to keep the family alive, then it is easy to understand why.

Among the interesting people who were part of my mother's life during that period of two and a half years of her maintaining Judy's Silver Shop, was a Blackfoot Indian man named Mr. Aliquah. I have no idea if Mr. Aliquah had any other name, first or last, because everyone in the family simply called him Mr. Aliquah. He was probably in his late 50s when my mother ran her shop. He had his own antique shop on the corner near the end of the Plaza, some distance from my mother's shop. He advertised that he bought silver and gold and he operated the shop from a very large office desk centered deep inside, not far from his own extremely large safe, painted with an Indian in a full Hollywood style headdress. His space was much larger than my mother's, and the walls were hung up to the ceiling with paintings, hanging sculpture, prints, and anything that he thought would attract attention. Each of the side walls held glass-fronted showcases with small artifacts from all over the world. For a young person, this was like a museum.

Mr. Aliquah was enigmatic, but warm and interesting. He was about five feet six inches, a rotund man with a shirt and tie, a dark jacket and trousers all somewhat rumpled and comfortable. His skin looked sunburned, with deep ridges around his mouth. He was clean shaven, with gray hair closely cropped. His eyes were intense, his lips full, with always a quizzical expression. I thought he was wonderful in part because he was the most exotic person I knew, and I felt enormously satisfied by the knowledge that he was a good friend of my family and also a good friend to me.

He often showed me interesting pieces in his collection, and often let me hold them and ask questions about them. One of his most peculiar habits was to chew rather than smoke his cigars. While we sat and talked, he would chew the tobacco and pull out the bottom drawer of his desk, which held a spittoon, and lean over to expectorate a chew before starting a new one. I had never seen anyone do this before, but somehow it did not seem bizarre to me. Everyone in my family smoked all the time, and I was always around cigarettes and cigars. My uncle Richard dressed windows using large cardboard "statues" of the Philip Morris Bellboy, who "called for Philip Morris." The cigarette company employed my uncle Richard, so there were packages of Philip Morris cigarettes in the house at all times. They did not interest me enough to want to smoke, although I took all the smoking in the family for granted, as did everyone else.

Mr. Aliquah's shop was on my way home from school, and often before I would visit with my mother, I would stop and talk with him. He was extremely cordial to me and treated me as if I were a legitimate person, not just a twelve year-old. I asked him lots of questions and got very few direct answers. I did learn that he had come from Oklahoma or some place close to Oklahoma and that he lived alone in a nearby hotel on Harrison Street from which he walked to his shop. He never drove a car and would never accept a ride from my father, explaining to me that he rarely drove in a car with anyone. I asked him why that was true and he explained that if it was a person's fate to be killed in an accident he did not want to share that fate by being in the car with him. I thought that was interesting, although it never affected my own willingness to drive in cars. Mr. Aliquah had many curious superstitions but they never affected me because fate was not something I could take seriously even though Mr. Aliquah could be at times persuasive.

The period of my mother's joy was quite wonderful. She was radiant, cheerful, and filled with hope in a way that I had not seen before. Unfortunately, because I was so young and so tied up with all the things I was doing in school and all my own personal interests, I did not fully understand her delight or what her experiences meant to her. I was now working steadily with my Gilbert Chemistry Set trying to experiment with all the permutations and combinations that were available to me at home. I often spent an afternoon demonstrating various minor marvels to my grandmother Helena – a captive audience by now – with my chemistry set. She was easy to please and I know now that simply having some form of entertainment in her room was enough to please her. She had no radio, and television was not yet available, so it is painful for me now to think how restricted her last years were.

Unfortunately, *Judy's Silver Shop* did not last long. After two and a half years my mother had to close her shop to take care of my grandmothers who were both, by then, in bed permanently. Everything changed one summer night when my grandmother Margaret went across the street, as she often did, to Mrs. Breitenbach's house to sit on the porch and talk with the women who gathered there. She would walk over after dinner many evenings in the summer months, and it seemed to be a genuine time of cheer for her. But that night Mrs. Breitenbach and two other women walked her slowly home and up to our porch and rang the bell. I answered the door and saw my grandmother being held steady by these women. She had a stunned look on her face and could barely whisper.

My parents got her upstairs to her room and into her bed, but what we did not know is that she had had a massive stroke. It paralyzed her on her left side, and made it difficult for her to speak. She knew who we were, but she could not get out of bed, and she could not feed herself. This was a catastrophe and robbed my mother of the one great joy of her life: her independence.

Margaret's stroke confined her to bed and signaled the end of *Judy's Silver Shop*. My mother closed the doors reluctantly--probably heartbroken--and spent her days in the house looking after both sick women. She was devastated by the loss of the one thing that was distinctly hers and at which she was extraordinarily good.

At home I pitched in to help in every way that I could, but the overall responsibility fell on her shoulders. She did not make my father's life easy throughout this period. She was bitter and angry and let him know how unhappy she was. Ernest tried to explain that the silver shop might have closed anyway. The economy was not as good that year as he had hoped and people were not buying high quality silver the way they had in the first years of the shop's existence. Something had happened to the business and the shop might have fallen victim to economic change no matter what. In addition to this consolation, he pitched in and tried to do all he could to help both my grandparents.

By this time, early 1949, Aunt Jett and uncle Alfred had been out of the house for some time. Now there were just my parents, my grandmothers, and me. But with the grandmothers in bed we were all grounded. We could never leave the house together except to sit in the evenings on the front porch. Friends visited us occasionally. And sometimes we would have people in for card parties. My mother became a whiz at Canasta, although I had to learn the game first and teach it to her. My father, an exceptional card player, looked down his nose at the game, but he participated in order to be sociable. Although he was a good card player he never liked to see me play cards. He never knew that earlier, during a summer vacation, Alfred and I used to play cards all day long, day after day.

While she nursed my grandmothers, Julia tried to make good use of her time. She was passionate about making clothes. Her Singer sewing machine was set up in the downstairs sewing room near the large walk-in closet and she bought patterns and fabric for suits, jackets, dresses, and coats. When she wasn't sewing she was knitting, and she draped the knitting yarn over my outstretched arms while she rolled it into a usable ball for her operations. Most of her clothing was well tailored and conservative. Unfortunately, I sometimes inadvertently discouraged her from wearing what she made.

Once she produced a fine looking suit in a light green-gray wool. It had a round collar, and an Audrey Hepburn flair to the jacket and skirt. My mother worked on it for weeks and when she finished she put the garment on and examined herself in the mirror. "How does it look?" she asked me. "Great," I said. "I like it." "Does it look homemade?" she asked. And offering what I thought was my highest praise, I nodded and said, "Yes." That did it. She took the suit off and never wore it again.

During this period my mother surprised everyone by deciding to learn to play my grandfather's piano. She loved Carmen Cavallaro, bought his instruction book, and found a piano teacher who came to the house. She made some progress but could never quite get the hang of it. Her sense of rhythm was undeveloped, and her playing was stiff and unnatural. But she did learn one popular piece, "Alice Blue Gown," which she played again and again for over a year. She was never discouraged, and always hopeful that sooner or later she would learn, but it never happened. During the years when my grandmothers were in bed, she took a lesson a week. I took lessons briefly as well and tried to help her, but neither of us was destined to play the piano.

When my grandmothers were in their invalid beds, my mother often talked on the phone incessantly. She was like a modern teenager. Her conversations would last the better part of an hour. She belonged to several women's business associations. She was the treasurer of the Quota Club, a group of East Orange business women who met at the Hotel Suburban on Harrison Street to listen to uplifting talks about how to succeed in business. Many of these women had problems and in those days people did not go to counselors or psychiatrists. Instead they talked to my mother and unloaded everything on her. My mother would get the call, then put the phone down for a moment, get her package of Chesterfields and pull up a chair and start smoking and nodding and "Ooohing." Everything was a crisis and she would sometimes talk confidentially into the receiver for hours on end.

Often she would feel rotten at the end of these calls. I didn't understand at first, but I soon caught on and told her that it was unfair for people to unload their grief and leave her depressed. But she took call after call and soon became an informal counselor to a half dozen other women. In some ways this must have helped her and must have helped them. Today a modern organization with a training manual is devoted to the principle of co-counseling, but I think that when my mother was involved it was one-way traffic only. She got no help from the people on the other end of the line.

This might have been harmless if she had not gotten repeated calls from a woman who drank. She was also a member of the Quota Club and needed a sympathetic listener. For several Saturdays she would call and drink while she talked and threaten suicide over her troubles. She was in her forties, pleasant enough, smart, and quite independent. But she committed suicide one Saturday after hanging up from a long phone session. My mother never dreamed the woman would go through with it, but she turned on the gas and lay down in the kitchen to die. My mother felt responsible for months afterwards. Perhaps ever afterwards.

One failure looms large. Because of her accident, because of the stubbornness of the Ford Model A, or because of her lack of coordination, she could not learn to drive. Teaching my mother to drive was a cross that my father bore for several years and it became mine as well. My father tried to teach my mother how to drive for at least three summers. I sat in the rumble seat and listened to the gnashing of teeth and gears in the front of the car. My mother got it going, jolted us into gear with a stuttering pummeling and moved at a snail's pace forward in a large empty parking lot only to fail to move to the next gear or to suddenly stand on the brakes in fear. When she got the car going she could not steer it right or left while keeping her foot on the gas. The result was that in negotiating the turns the car would lurch rabidly forward and I would hit every available surface in the back of the machine while my father's panicked voice would grow louder and louder until he would suddenly lean over and grab the wheel to avert a tree, a car, a disaster.

At those moments my mother complained loudly that he wasn't helping and that she could have gotten the car straightened out. But it was the only car they had and it was not insured against destruction. We would go out for two or three hours at a time, on a grand day, in a remote location. Then my mother would drive, at approximately ten miles an hour for the first half of the lesson, then when she got more confident she would move up to about twenty miles an hour. For part of the time she would seem to do well. My father would shower praise on her while they drove and I would add my praise when we got home. But these sessions always produced a moment of crisis when my mother would panic and the car would suddenly lurch in the wrong gear and stall out. Starting the car was never easy, and my mother often became unglued trying to restart the overheated engine.

After years of failure my father suggested that she try a driving school and she did. The school had modern cars with automatic transmissions, and that made a difference. She got up to thirty miles an hour and steered around corners and gave the appearance of a competent driver. But she had her problems there, too. She took months to get to the point at which the instructor felt he could take her for her license. Finally the day arrived. When she went for her license she thought she was going to make it. But the licensor asked her to parallel park and he was none too patient with her. She became rattled and ran up on the curb, then backed into a car, stalled out, and generally revealed her mountainous fear and failed the test. She never went back again.

She never forgave my father or me for her failure to learn to drive. When I was in my fifties I heard her accuse me of not having taught her how to drive. I realize today that one of the legacies of being my mother's child is the sense of guilt attached with not living up to her expectations. She was a skilled producer of guilt and an even more skilled producer of expectations. She expected good behavior and always told me to get something or do something "like a good boy." That was a litany of my childhood. "Get me my glasses like a good boy." "Go over and see if your grandmother needs you like a good boy." "Help me with the knitting today like a good boy." It never ended. I did my best to be a good boy but I'm sure it was never enough.

Ernest Jr. and the Amazing Daily Double

Late in his life, my father and I had almost no small talk between us. Even our most casual conversations eventually moved toward questions about the hereafter, Darwinism, and moral justice. Whether in the shadow of the porch, on long distance telephone, or walking down Harrison Street, we always came back to the soul and the nature of God. If we were suddenly to speak again now, forty years after his death, I am sure his first words would be, "Didn't I tell you?"

Meanwhile, however, I had to grow into such conversations. When I was a very young child my father was the center of my life, all the more so because he spent so much time out of sight. He commuted to New York from East Orange for thirty-seven years. Sometimes he reviewed a typical day's travel, citing the railroad, the ferry, the subway, the bus, and a brisk walk up several flights of stairs. On summer evenings I waited on the corner of Webster Place and Harrison Street, sometimes climbing the street sign and sitting on its top until he arrived. I expected him at 7:04, but he often showed up at 7:22, or even later. He and I then walked together up the street talking away about what we did that day. Once in the

My father and I in 1944.
The Model A Roadster is in the background

house he hung his jacket on the full length mirror and headed into the kitchen to see my mother.

During his summer vacations, he often took me to New York on the ferry from Hoboken. He photographed me near the shark tanks at the Art Deco Aquarium in the Battery when I was six years old. We visited many of his customers in their workshops where I once met an older man who spent his life fashioning silver coffee pots. Arthritis and repetitive work deformed and gnarled his hands. Yet, he was a gracious soul who let me hold the item he was working on and explained how he was able to get the shapes of flowers and leaves to stand out in the design. My father knew him because for years he sold him the silver materials that went into his work.

On our visits to the Metropolitan Museum of Art, my father took special interest in older paintings, impressed by the grandness of other people's lives. He would stand in front of a Rembrandt and point out the unusual clothes that people wore and help me marvel at the details and accuracy of the portraits. Although he definitely appreciated the skill of the artist, he was not really interested in the paintings as art, so much as he was interested in them as records of history. Among the things that fascinated him were the contemporary similarities with people in years gone by, the way they looked much like people of today, the way some of the faces reminded him of people he knew. The fabrics in the paintings were rich, richer than any he had seen in our world, which made him realize that there was a strong contrast between the richness and wealth of the people in these paintings and the ordinariness of our daily lives. Somehow, he was able to take this in his stride and not react in a way that depressed him. Naturally he took special interest in paintings with gold and silver goblets and tankards, with jewels and ornamental precious metal objects. He understood them better than anything else he saw in the paintings. The furnished rooms from other centuries interested him, too. He studied older clothes presses, side tables, chairs, and every day acoutrements that he may have hoped to see in some of the homes he visited on estate sales. I enjoyed these excursions when I was young, but in later life I realized how much they contributed to my own intellectual development.

One curious detail I recall was his studying a fifteenth century painting of a group of figures in a palace setting. Their garments were remarkable, the setting courtly, and the faces clearly those of the royal families. But in the lower center of the painting, on a marble balustrade, was a perfectly painted blue-bottle fly. I looked at the painting and did not make much of it, but he was absolutely fascinated by the fly not because it was so accurately painted, but because the fly in the fifteenth century was precisely like the fly he saw in his own backyard. It had not changed at all, and that for him was surprising. I took a closer look and marveled as well.

We spent quite a bit of time in museums in New York largely, I think, because he had never been able to spend any time in them when he was my age. I think he was contributing to my education on one level, but on another and maybe more important level he was extending his own education. The works he saw sharpened his eye for those times when he went out on "buys," looking for bargains in the estate sales in the wealthy neighborhoods that surrounded us. As he once said to me, "Museums are good, but they're limited. You can't buy anything in them." And given his talents, I can see that might have curtailed his pleasure even in the Metropolitan Museum of Art.

In some ways, Ernest was simple in his pleasures. He ate his dinner while telling my mother the office news, focusing on personalities and the health of the business. He spoke about his boss, Mr. Spiess and his co-worker, Warren, whom he had recruited for Handy & Harman. After dinner we all listened to the radio the way people watch television today. We followed a regular pattern of shows on their appropriate evenings, "Mr. Keen, Tracer of Lost Persons," "The Shadow," "Duffy's Tavern," "Amos and Andy," "The Jack Benny Show," and many others. They gave us pleasure, just by virtue of our being able to laugh and talk back at the shows' silliness or seriousness. My father always listened closely to "Walter Winchell," "Lowell Thomas," "Fulton Lewis, Jr.," "Drew Pearson," "H. V. Kaltenborn," and other news commentators, probably giving them too much credit for their opinions.

My father rarely got angry, but when he did people watched out. Only once did he have to swat me. It happened in our kitchen when I was about nine, and whatever I was doing, I never did it again. Like most men of that generation, when I was little he did not make a point of telling me he loved me. He expected me to understand his love without his having to point it out. Much later, however, in the decade before he died, he expressed his affection openly, and we made it clear how much we loved each other.

The nuns at St. John's School beat my father, a natural lefty, until he could write as fluently with his right hand as with his left. As a result he was awkward and not much of an athlete. He had no interest in any sport except horse racing, if that qualifies. That meant we did not go out in the tiny green space between our house and the next door neighbor's to play catch. At least not often, and never with success. I played baseball and football and shot baskets on the backboard up on the garage, but my father never took any interest in sports. And because only the rich played golf and tennis it never occurred to either of us that we might have enjoyed trying them. Instead, we shared another mutual pleasure: the movies.

I never went to the Saturday morning cartoons and serials that figured in the lives of so many kids in those years. Instead, my father and I went to the movies every Friday night, every Saturday night, and every Sunday afternoon for many years. We lived on a diet of double features and at the point of greatest suspense my father often leaned over and told me what the hero or villain would do next. It always amazed me that he knew what was about to happen.

We loved war movies with John Wayne, Ward Bond, and Pedro Armendarez in cowboy and Indian westerns by John Ford, suave urban mysteries with Boston Blackie or William Powell, and we never missed the Sherlock Holmes films with Basil Rathbone. We avoided musicals and romances except when my mother came along. At no time would we ever think to find out when a film began in order to see it from the beginning. We always went into a film in the middle, watched it to the end, sat through the second feature, then waited until the first feature reached the spot where we came in. Then we left. My father later talked about those years, from about my seventh to my thirteenth birthday, as having been wonderful because we spent so much time together. He had a difficult adjustment when I began taking girls to the movies.

We shared the memory of one of our funniest moments

in the Little Theater in Newark, a rerun house. We rarely went to the Little because it was far away and almost never had anything we hadn't seen. But this Sunday the Little showed *The Tales of the Bengal Lancers*, and my father made a stop on the street to buy a large bag of raw unshelled peanuts. Inside we split them open and tossed the shells so they rolled under the seats in front of us. We almost covered the floor when a group of latecomers passed in front of us crushing the shells loudly under foot. They stopped and glared at us in the dark. We sat mute, both on the verge of hysterics, but we didn't laugh until we drove home in our noisy Model A. We had been naughty and both us had great fun.

Two other wonderful adventure films made an impression on me in my early youth: *Drums Along the Mohawk*, and *Beau Geste*. I carried the images of the Viking's Funeral and the scene of one of the brothers shot in the leg with a cannon from their toy gun ship in *Beau Geste* in my imagination for forty years until I finally saw the film again as an adult on late night television. The years only slightly diminished its effect. I was six or seven when I saw those films originally, but they have remained vital images throughout my life. Many other films took on importance then, especially films made about World War II and even more especially, the newsreels of the war. *Guadalcanal Diary*, *Bataan*, and *They Were Expendable*, were great, but I also remember *Tarawa*, a bloody documentary of the Pacific war in vivid color. These were powerful films.

During my grade school years my father went out on "buys." He scanned the Newark Evening News to see which estates stood up for sale on a Saturday morning. These were not tag sales. Houses never put furniture, clothing, and bric a brac out on the lawn. Or, if they did, we never noticed them. We always found the goods inside.

When a house opened its doors people swarmed through, picked things up, asked a price and began to haggle. My father embarrassed me by bargaining mercilessly for various items. It was bad enough at these estate sales, but he even haggled in department stores. He would fit me out in a jacket or shoes down at Bamberger's and then say to the salesman, "What will you take for this." The salesman would point to the price tag in alarm, but my father would persist and I'd turn red with shame. However, he usually got the price down, and I have discovered that in my advanced years I have done the same.

We visited some wonderful homes. The mansions in South Orange, in West Orange, in Montclair, and in Llewellyn Park, Thomas Edison's amazing turn of the century living experiment, impressed us as much as the mansions we saw in the 1930s comedies with everyone in evening clothes. The furniture we bought was elegant and inexpensive. My father bought silver and jewelry, with a keen eye for a bargain. He loved good paintings and fine furniture, and we bought whatever we could fit into the Model A Roadster. I still have a beautiful walnut round table that we bought together, one of a pair. After we rushed our table home, we returned for its twin in vain. Looking back, I realize I treated his buys as adventures and I enjoyed the houses we visited. I never sought to buy anything for myself, but I shared my father's enthusiasm.

He kept a few of the finer pieces, although these excursions rarely resulted in treasures for ourselves. The point was to keep the items moving and make some money. My father was good at this. He had several reliable dealers who took whatever he wanted to sell, making a better profit themselves. He enjoyed a pure form of economic capitalism, albeit on a tiny scale. It made my father feel good to think that he could spot a bargain and make some money on it.

One house in Llewellyn Park stands out in my memory. Llewellyn Park was an experiment developed by a number of talented and wealthy people who took a large parcel of land in West Orange and kept it as it was when the Leni-Lenape Indians inhabited the region. They built lavish homes on considerable acreage, but barely disturbed the land. There were no extensive lawns. The primary road wound through astonishing natural redstone cliffs, stands of old cypress, yew, ash, elm, a profusion of juniper and pines and gigantic oaks and maples.

The house I remember best once belonged to Thomas Edison, although when we visited it was owned by a former Edison executive. The house seemed like a museum. I stood speechless in the library, which resembled the reading room in the Folger Library in Washington D.C. The cherry paneled bookshelves reached out into the room. Portraits of distinguished men, women, and boys hung on the walls above. The gentleman who showed us through shepherded me and pointed out some of the more important books. He paused in front of one of the paintings and asked me if I knew who it portrayed. I failed to recognize Thomas Edison as a young man, because he looked nothing like the balding older man who I knew lived somewhere in Florida. I still remember feeling like a peasant in that palatial grandeur, so close to where I lived, and yet so far away that it could have been in Versailles.

When I went to high school my father converted his Friday evenings to playing gin rummy behind McManus's liquor store on Central Avenue. He was a gifted card player because he had an iron-clad memory, especially for numbers, and he usually knew what cards everyone else held. He won much more than he lost.

He also went to Monmouth Race Track during his two-week summer vacation. We all heard about his adventures. Sometimes he went with his younger brother Paul and he would come home complaining about Paul's conservative betting. Paul ignored the Daily Double. We heard the details of every race, how this or that horse had almost won or had totally lost or, rarely, how it had paid off some money. The adventures sounded wonderful and I longed to go with him, but I was supposed to wait until I was sixteen.

At fourteen, and then six feet tall, I convinced my father to chance it, and we drove to Monmouth on the New Jersey shore for a day at the races. I stood up very straight as we approached the entrance ticket taker and got through easily. Then began the ritual my father always followed at the races. He had written down the last two numbers of his speedometer for the Daily Double. Then he reviewed the numbers that he spotted on the way down to the track to decide which of them repeated themselves and which might prove lucky. He promised me that I could bet two dollars on each race if I wanted to. So while he got in line at the Daily Double window I went down to look at the horses walking slowly along the railing prior to the first race. I had seen horses before, but not so close and not such wonderful, stately animals. I leaned on the railing exactly like the Black handler standing next to me.

Lee and Ernest in 1949

As I watched the horses parade by, the handler turned to me and said, "You see that big gray horse, boy?" I said I did. "That horse gonna win this race," he said. I didn't ask him why, nor did I ask him how he knew. I just stared at that huge, fine looking horse and decided I would put my first two dollars on it. So I walked back to find my father standing near the window checking his several Daily Double tickets. He made sure he covered all his bets. I said to him, "Dad, would you put two dollars on a horse for me?" He said "Sure, which one?" I had the number and gave it to him. He read the racing sheet and said the horse's name was Gay Song. I said, "Yes, and I want to play it to win." He tried to convince me to play it for place, but I insisted, and he put the bet in for me.

We then had only a few minutes to position ourselves to see the race, and we got there just as the horses left the gate. The noise and the yelling and the cheering from the crowd excited both of us. The horses made the first turn. Gay Song was in the middle of the pack. When they made the next turn one of my father's horses grabbed the lead. When they got to the stretch, Gay Song took over and moved out of the pack relentlessly forward, pounding on the track as if she had been toying rather than racing with her peers. The crowd roared. The man next to me held up his tickets and shouted in my ear. He jumped up on his seat and screamed. Gay Song won by three lengths. My father's Daily Double tickets were garbage. My horse, on the other hand, paid thirty-two dollars to win.

"How did you know?" my father asked. "How did you know about that horse?"

"Well," I told him, "this handler down by the railing just turned to me and said the horse was going to win the race."

"What?" he said. "Why didn't you tell me?" He got very excited. He couldn't believe his ears. "Why didn't you tell me?"

"I don't know," I said. "I didn't think of it."

My father almost lost it.

He couldn't imagine that I would get such privileged information and not pass it on as an inside tip. But it was my first horse race and my first bet. I have never been as lucky since, but then I don't have my father's passion for horses. It made a good story for a long time, although it would have made a better story if I had enough wits about me to tell the whole conversation at the time my father placed my bet.

About gambling, he was enthusiastic but never excessive. He always told me that "I owe them money," meaning he won more than he lost. No one in the family ever suffered because he lost a bet. When he won at the races he treated everyone to a dinner out. And in later years, he played the lottery hoping to win big.

I used to scoff at him for his fantasizing about the lottery. He said that when he hit it he would call me and make sure that all of us got a good share. He made sure Doris was covered, that I was covered, and that my mother was covered. We'd all share in the wealth. When I said I never bet on the lotto myself, he explained it to me. "How is somebody like me ever to get any money except by winning the lottery?" He was right. He spent twenty years retired and while he loved the idea of being paid for doing nothing, he always made sure he had a ticket on the lottery. And sometimes he won a few dollars. Never the big one.

In early middle age my father tried to figure out ways to make a few dollars and change our life. It never worked, but he kept trying. He had idea after idea for inventions that I see now were essentially crackpot schemes. He would describe the ideas for me and I would nod as if I understood what he was talking about. Most were vague proposals, but one came to fruition. He invented a device that held your telephone up in the air while leaving your hands free to write. It was a Rube Goldberg contraption with a weighted bottom and angled metal rods attached to the conventional receiver of the day. Because it attached to the telephone base it required no additional desk space. My father hired a lawyer, contacted a manufacturer, spent quite a bit of money and got a detailed mechanical drawing and a patent. That week in the New York Times we saw a simple device for sale that made it possible to balance a telephone on your shoulder, leaving you free to write. It cost $2.50.

In social situations my father liked to dominate a conversation. His themes were politics, religion, real estate, and the economy. People seemed to enjoy hearing him, although not all of them took him seriously. He especially loved predictions, and for a year before Pearl Harbor he predicted that the United States was definitely going to war with Japan. He never doubted it, but his friends never took him seriously and then added insult to injury by pretending not to remember that he had predicted it all along.

Later, when I started to question his behavior in dominating conversations with friends, I realized that part of it stemmed from his constant reading. He knew more than most of his friends, and they usually learned something from him. His brothers, of course, paid no attention to him. He gave them advice relentlessly, but none of them followed it. I often ignored his advice, too, but almost always at my peril.

Another fault involved dominating my mother--at times. One could not easily dominate my mother. As one of my cousins once said to me, "Just like in my family where my father is the boss, in your family your mother is the boss." Well, that was true in virtually every day to day affair, but in the larger issues of life, my father dominated. He understood money, for example, and he understood taxes and liabilities and how to buy real estate and how to spot good values, and he made every effort to teach some of these things to my mother, but she refused to take an interest. She let him deal with these things and after struggling to make her aware of their significance and to understand how they worked, he gave up.

Late in life he developed a strange vanity concerning the Jacobus name. He knew it was Dutch and assumed that his family had been in New Jersey since the early seventeenth century. When one of the commercial genealogical outfits promised to give him details about the family name for $40 he sent in his money and told me the information was on its way. Skeptical as ever, I scoffed at the whole idea. When the material arrived he showed it to me. Apparently the Jacobuses did not arrive in 1611, which disappointed him. But one detail was amazing. This outfit provided a four-color coat of arms suitable for framing. What it showed was a blue field on which, poised diagonally, were three silver ingots. My father's profession seemed linked to his genes.

Finally, my father disappointed me sometimes because he started to become a sentimentalist. He fished for sentimental responses the way other people fish for compliments (which my mother did constantly). He annoyed me one evening the year before he died when I scoffed at something he said that invited a sentimental reaction. He said to me, "You'll miss me when I'm gone." Of course it was true, but I wasn't about to give him the satisfaction of our ruminating on his death—especially since at age eighty-four he was doing fine. I was on the phone at the time and all I said was, "Look Dad, I miss you right now." I didn't give him the questionable pleasure of getting me into that sentimental corner musing on his mortality.

He knew the truth, though. I would give a great deal to have another eye to eye talk with him. I have not been able to listen to the few audio tapes I made of his conversation or to look at the few home videos in which he appears. I will do both one of these days, but right now I don't have the emotional courage to face either. Only recently I told a group of people about my father's saying I would miss him when he was gone and involuntarily I burst into tears, unable to hold back the emotion even for a few moments. He was right about a lot of things and he was especially right about that.

My Uncle, the Gay Bank Robber

I have jokingly referred to my Uncle Eddy as our bank robber. Trouble is, it's not a joke.

He was born several months after his father died and he was given his father's name. He was, therefore, my mother's youngest brother and in some ways--and I base this partly on the way she spoke of him and partly on my own observation--she was a mother to him. They were close throughout life and, of all her family, my mother seemed to worry most about Eddy. She spoke of him with great tenderness and concern, as if she felt that he might have a hard time taking care of himself. And even when there was nothing she could do for him, no way she could possibly be of genuine or effective assistance, she was anxious to help.

Physically, he resembled the picture I have of his father, but he was more slender, less physically prepossessing. He was a handsome man of about five-ten or so, with sandy hair, a winning smile, and a soft, velvety voice. His language was accurate, clear, and uncluttered with slang or colloquialisms, and when I was very young I found him pleasant to listen to. He

told me a few stories with a natural narrative sheen that added
dimension to his words.

Uncle Eddy Byrne

Eddy never lived with us on Webster Place. He spent
most of his life with his mother on White Street. He was
nothing at all like his brothers Uncle Billy and Uncle Robby.
They were rough and tough, both in their speech and their walk.
Eddy was more genteel, more reserved, more like my mother.

My mother and Eddy could hold an intelligent conversation without tempers flying and without voices being raised.

Eddy did not have Uncle Bill's sense of humor, and he did not have the party sense or rowdy streak that marked both Uncle Bill and his wife Aunt Betty. When he spoke, his voice was quiet, his pacing thoughtful and steady, his ideas carefully expressed and complete. He had little or no formal education beyond a few years of secondary school, but he was, like my mother, a reader. Unlike her, his reading was more literary. He once told me when I was in college that he read James Joyce's *Ulysses*. I hope that was true. He had a good mind and it was a genuine loss that he could not have trained it to some professional use.

I have the impression that Eddy was always delicate, especially in health. People in the family always worried over him. Even Uncle Bill and his son, Little Billy, worried about him. I'm surprised in retrospect to realize that Uncle Bill rarely if ever mentioned Uncle Eddy except to my mother. He never spoke to me about him and neither did Little Billy. Perhaps I should not be surprised. However, in a family that talked so much, Uncle Eddy should have come up in the conversation more often than he did. Such silence may have been a result of people's uneasiness in relation to him. He was different and not easy to fathom.

As a child I really liked Uncle Eddy. There was something about him that was appealing--I think it was that he was always engaged in what was happening in the world at large--he had a scope in his thinking that was unusual, a scope that brought in the world around him. He was more than what one saw on the surface, whereas Uncle Bill was always just what you saw. Uncle Bill was not, as Margaret would have put it, "still waters running deep." Uncle Eddy, on the other hand, seemed to have depths suggesting an intellectual and emotional richness that was not especially evident in other members of the family. Such a judgment must be taken with some caution, naturally, especially since it was made by a very young person long ago. I am not sure how I would react to Uncle Eddy today. I rather hope I would have the same view, but such judgments are difficult to interpret from a distance of years. Suffice it to say that Eddy had charm and grace. I enjoyed hearing him talk and I enjoyed seeing him when he visited.

I have absolutely no memory of Uncle Eddy in my real childhood, the years between age three and age eight. By that I mean only that I do not recall his spending time with me the way, for example, my father's brother,Uncle Paul, and Doris's Howard Cullen did. So many people were in my life in those early years that they made me feel the world was rich and filled with exciting things to do and to talk about. Uncle Eddy does not have a real place in my life until after the end of World War II.

Before the war Eddy was able to get a job as a bank messenger for the First National Bank of Montclair. This was a signal moment in his life because it represented a real job with a real opportunity for advancement. He seems to have done well at the job and took special pride in his work.

Since I have no memories of him between 1937 and 1942, I can only infer what he must have been like. Doris naturally remembers him and thinks of him as a gentle and loving man. They were close because Doris spent a good deal of time with Margaret, and Eddy lived with Margaret steadily until the war. Doris remembered Eddy helping to teach her how to tie her shoes. He also made up wonderful stories for her, including one about a chocolate Victrola that Doris liked to have him tell over and over. From what she says, it was a story rich in detail and full of delight. Doris associated him with his ambitions to write and mentioned that he left behind a small collection of writings in the basement of 22 Webster Place before the war. That did not survive our many moves.

Given his gentleness and intellectuality, it seems out of character for Uncle Eddy, but some time between 1937 and 1940 he was given a courier package with money destined for another bank in Newark. He was given clear instructions and sent on his mission. Somewhere along the way he decided not to deliver the money. Instead, he decided to go to New York and to get a room in Times Square and live the high life. It was a Friday and he doubted anyone would miss him. So he took a room in a cheap hotel and went out on the town. He had over four thousand dollars in his satchel and thought he could do some wonderful things with that much money.

Fortunately, he was found almost immediately. By Monday he was in custody, marched back to Newark, where he was detained in the local lockup. His picture appeared in the Newark *Star-Ledger* where Doris remembers having seen it. He had spent almost forty dollars of the swag. As far as my sister and I can remember, he did not go to jail. This was a difficult time in America for many young men, and the judge must have offered the same deal to a number of them. He told Eddy he could do time or join the army. He had his choice. Uncle Eddy did not much like the idea of being in the army, but he liked the idea of jail even less. So he found himself a private in the military reserve. He seems not to have been called into active service until later, after the war broke out.

The anxiety that event produced must have rocked the family. Margaret could not have imagined her youngest child would do anything untoward, and the thought of him as a bank robber must have sent her into a paroxysm of guilt and shame. My mother, too, must have been in agony. They both loved Eddy and would have no idea how to help him. My mother was straightforward enough in later years to tell me that he had taken money from the bank and that he had been caught, but she never talked about what she and her mother must have gone through trying to sort out the emotions aroused by this event. She also never gave me enough details to thoroughly understand what had really happened--why, for example, Eddy thought he could get away with it. Her attitude was shaped by her own sense of denial.

Another aspect of Eddy's behavior might help me understand him a little better. As I said, he was very intelligent, but not very well educated. He had an intellectual reach, but not enough intellectual grasp. He had in his youth--and through much of the time I knew him--a fixation on Napoleon. Doris has told me that he had a French flag on the wall and that he had a number of books on Napoleon. He talked about Napoleon a great deal and obviously admired him and his great European campaigns. Napoleon was his man and he emulated him in whatever ways he could. Such behavior is almost comically associated with crazy people, but Eddy was not crazy, at least not certifiably. And my conversations with him in the later 1940s and early 1950s indicated that he was sane and normal. He was an enthusiast, but not a nut.

However, in the period before the war Eddy seems to have taken up with some kind of paramilitary group. It is difficult for me to comprehend how this could have happened, but while he was in the army, he also seems to have been associated with proto-Fascist groups in Newark or New York. I have no memory of this. However, Doris remembers that he would on occasion visit our grandmother at our house at 22 Webster Place before the war wearing very fancy dark military uniforms. During the day at this time, he worked for the Western Union delivering telegrams and he wore a uniform there, too. But the uniforms he wore when he visited Webster Place--late at night, around eleven o'clock--were, as Doris said, "like a general's uniform, with plenty of braids, jodhpurs, and a fancy large hat." This sounds to me very much like the uniforms that the German Bunds wore when they met in the hills of northern New Jersey before the war. The fanciness and the Napoleonic order would have appealed to Eddy, although I am confident that he never really understood the political implications of what he was doing. When I knew him in later years he never alluded to this part of his life and he only rarely referred to political issues.

One of the questions that both my sister and I have in common regarding Eddy concerns his possible homosexuality. He never had a woman in his personal life. Doris felt that there was a man who had influenced Eddy when Eddy was very young and who might have been responsible for his "criminal" tendencies. She had no idea who this man was or how he could have gotten to know him. She felt that he misled Eddy and that Eddy might not have done some of the bizarre things he did if this man had left Eddy alone. My father was very specific regarding him because he was certain that Eddy was homosexual. He quizzed me carefully when I was in my teens about the way Uncle Eddy behaved when he was near me, and asked me whether or not he ever did anything to molest me. He never did, and I was rather surprised at the thought that he might. It did not change my thinking about Uncle Eddy and it did not make me like him less. It was just a strange and extraordinary thing in my life and I accepted it as a fact rather than worrying about it.

When the war began, Eddy was called up and into service. For a while, the army benefitted Eddy in a number of ways. For one thing, it gave him the structure he needed to keep his life focused and to avoid the kind of problems he must have faced when he ran off to Times Square. Before he went overseas, he was stationed at Fort Dix along with thousands of other New Jersey soldiers. He visited us on his leaves in a sharply pressed uniform looking bright, confident, cheerful.

During some of this time, Eddy's life grew complicated and he suffered a setback. What I remember most vividly was being in the front yard of our rented house in Sanford Street one afternoon in 1943 when a khaki military sedan pulled up to the front walkway and two Military Policemen in full uniform, with weapons and baton, marched up to the front door and rang the bell. They ignored me entirely. I was eight years old and I rose from the grass and followed them inside. What I heard them telling my mother was that Uncle Eddy had gone Absent Without Leave, which meant he was a criminal. Again. My mother and grandmother were anxious for him. They had no idea where he was. The MPs explained that Eddy would be put in the stockade when he was found. We were told to report him to the authorities the minute we heard anything from him.

When he was found, he lost his stripes, did a few weeks in the stockade, then discovered that he was being shipped out. He wound up in Italy. He sent letters back to our house. Everyone depended on V-Mail in those days, and we always wanted to know what Eddy was doing. Of course, we were mostly anxious to be sure that Eddy was not hurt or killed. Luckily, Eddy was a good typist and used his skills throughout the war typing up reports and letters. He became a corporal and eventually found himself stationed in Trieste. I knew of Trieste primarily because I collected stamps and had associated Trieste with Fiume, "countries" I could only imagine in terms of postage rather than geography. It was from Trieste that Eddy sent us some souvenirs carefully crated. Curiously, I have no idea now what the souvenirs were--I remember only a few pieces of bric-a-brac--but I still have a piece of wood from the crate.

Trieste was important in literature if only because James Joyce lived there for many years while he wrote *A Portrait of the Artist as a Young Man*. But there were other literary figures in Trieste, and it was a city important to Italy, Austria, and Hungary. Today it appears sleepy and bourgeois. It was not important in the war, and Eddy probably had a good time there. He was himself never a successful literary person--his letters were unremarkable, although sometimes a bit whimsical and strange. But he was interested in intellectual things and must have found enough people in Trieste to talk with seriously. Now, after having visited Trieste myself, I would like to know whether he was aware of its historical importance and its artistic background. Neither of my parents had heard of Trieste. All they knew was that Eddy would remain there for some time, until the end of the war.

After the war Eddy stayed on as a career army man. He had no calling, no preparation for civilian life, and no reason to change what he was doing. I can understand how he would have evaluated his situation. The army guaranteed him meals, clothing, housing, and pay. No where in civilian life could those things have come his way without a great deal of struggle. Surely, he could not come back to New Jersey and his family after having been through Europe and having seen something of the world. His mother lived with us, so he could not count on a home while he sorted things out. The army was his logical move.

When he visited after the war he usually showed up in his uniform, looking very smart and dignified. He earned back some of his stripes and even rose to the rank of sergeant. The army sent him to the Pacific in the early 1950s and he weathered through a typhoon when he was on Iwo Jima. He told me that he had been in a relatively open bunker of some sort during the storm and that the wind speed indicator that had been erected on the island to measure such storms was jammed at one hundred seventy-five miles an hour. He said it was an act of God that he was not washed away in the storm.

The years in the early 1950s were relatively stable for Eddy. He maintained his fixations and his interests. He read a great many books. And now and then we would get a letter. Unfortunately, he ran into trouble in the army again while he was in the Pacific. He was court-marshaled for an act of insubordination. In 1955 or so my mother gave me the official army papers to examine in an effort to see if there was a way we could appeal the case. I examined them in detail and discovered that the primary charges against Uncle Eddy were based on insults he had hurled against his superior officer. Among the things he told his Captain were that "I'd rather be in the Russian Army than in the American Army."

A number of other such outbursts were noted in these papers, but there was relatively little that I thought was actionable. For example, he was not guilty of brawling, theft, sexual misconduct, or anything that involved a serious infraction of the law. The primary complaints against him concerned his attitude and his unwillingness to cooperate with his commandant. The result was that the court found him guilty and sentenced him to short time in the stockade and granted him a dishonorable discharge. We appealed the case, but on what basis I cannot imagine. I also remember that the appeal was denied. Doris told me that she thought the charges against him were later dropped and his discharge was made honorable. As a result, she says, there was a flag on his coffin. However, I doubt this. The funeral home would have placed the flag on his coffin just by virtue of his having been a veteran. They would never have known of his dishonorable discharge.

Doris remembered visiting Eddy in prison in New York in 1958 or 1959, shortly after he had been discharged. Uncle Eddy had lived for a while with Little Billy down in Belmar, and Billy assured Doris that they would "shape him up." However, Doris also remembers that Little Billy had his hands full with him and could not really handle him. There was some dispute between them--Little Billy never mentioned any of this to me--and Uncle Eddy wound up moving to New York City. Doris did not recall why Eddy was in prison. She remembered that he was not there for a long time. She brought him a toothbrush, tooth paste, and a few other things he needed. I suspect that he may have been arrested for disorderly conduct, drunkenness, or resisting an officer, or all three.

The years he was in New York were difficult for him. He lived on Third Avenue down in or near Alphabet City, a rough area then. He was by this time a very heavy drinker and drunk much of the time. He would call our house at various times of day, early afternoon, late in the evening, whenever the spirit moved him. Sometimes he wanted money. He asked my mother for money during almost all these conversations. She may have given him some. Uncle Eddy was to my mother what Uncle Jack was to my father: a cross that one never stopped bearing.

I spoke with him because I was usually the one who answered the phone. At first I hardly knew what to make of these phone calls. He might mention Napoleon and tell me something interesting, but in the late conversations, he would go off on ramblings and ravings about the next war. "During the next war, Tucker, I'm going to make you a field marshal in charge of the Panzer Corps. That's right. You can have the African command, like Rommel." Such language baffled me, especially since hyperbole would fly without restraint. He had no sense of who I was, what I thought, or what my values were. He was a complete egoist at this time and saw everyone else in terms of a projection of his own ego. I was for him an instrument, and nothing more. I talked with him when he was stone drunk and I tried to reason with him, but it was clear that he didn't hear me. He didn't care what I thought or felt, and he certainly did not care what my mother thought or felt.

Concerning my father, he was cautious because it was plain

that my father refused to take him seriously. Indeed, my father was deeply suspicious of him and thought of him as a very unreliable character. What my father knew that Eddy did not is the pain that Eddy caused my mother. Because she was so powerless to help or to change Eddy, my mother agonized over his bizarre behavior and his painful late phone calls. Somehow Eddy could not take care of himself and he could not stay out of trouble.

His death on November 29, 1960 is a mystery that I must some day unravel. According to Doris and my mother, Uncle Eddy died in the winter of pneumonia. Doris said that Little Billy assured her that he was in the hospital "with the nuns" when they declared him dead from this disease. However, my father told me specifically that Eddy was murdered. He said he went with the New York City Police to his apartment on Third Avenue where he had been strangled with a wet towel. My father said he was living with a homosexual man and that the death had been the result of some kind of sexual dispute. My father told me he had to clean the place up and get Eddy's things and that he could not tell my mother the awful truth about his violent end.

Frankly, I don't know what to believe. Uncle Eddy was such an unusual and strange man that it is possible that either story is true. In other words, it is possible that he was almost killed by someone, then found and put into a hospital where he died. The pneumonia spin could have been put on this later to protect the family and to accomplish the symmetry of having young Eddy die of the same disease that killed his father. Families protect themselves, especially when reflecting on such people as my Uncle Eddy.

My sense of it all concerns Eddy and his opportunities, which were painfully restricted because of his circumstances and the stage of development of the nation itself. If Eddy had been born twenty years later, say in 1935, he would have been able to go to college and develop his intellect. His homosexuality may still have had to be hidden, but not forever, and it would not have been thought a criminal aspect of personality. In other words, even if he were a bit eccentric, he might have had a chance at life. I knew and liked him, and I think he deserved a better chance than he got.

Santa's Burglars: Robbed on Christmas Eve

Ernest and Julia always managed, no matter what the circumstances, to be original and even sumptuous in our Christmas decorations and celebrations. Church was always a central ingredient of the holiday season, and in the Sundays approaching the big day, the priests would read us segments of the Gospels involving the coming birth of Christ. Even in my public elementary school, when we read a portion of the Bible each morning, we would focus on the entries in the New Testament that foreshadowed Christ's birth. In school we would also have dramatic pageants that included the Holy Family done more or less the same way each year. Naturally, we would sing Christmas Carols. I loved those musical classes more than any other. My parents knew little about the ways in which our school participated in the general holiday celebrations, and what they did know they more or less accepted without criticism. They had been church schooled themselves, so our plays and songs and readings would have seemed scant compared with what they themselves must have experienced as children.

I mention the sermons in the church, and the general

holiday festivities in the school because each of them emphasized the spiritual values that Christians associate with Christmas. I realize that none of what I experienced in public school would be possible for today's students. And sometimes I wonder what my Jewish classmates made of it all. They rarely if ever seemed annoyed or offended by what went on, but that does not mean that they were pleased with it, or that they were not in fact hurt by feeling left out or even, possibly threatened. It is possible – perhaps likely – that some parents protested. But if so, such protests did not filter down to me.

What I enjoyed most was the chance to sing Christmas Carols in my music class. Curiously, of all the curriculum opportunities at Nassau School, where I went to first grade, then from third to eighth grade, the best were the arts classes and the music classes. But the music classes stand out as having been pure pleasure. They were not entirely superficial fun, either. They were often filled with important academic content. We sang many folk songs from Eastern Europe, from South America, from Asia, from Canada, and from the American South as well as the mid-west and far west. In addition, we often sang songs in foreign languages, German, French, Italian, Spanish, and Latin. The Latin songs, such as Ave Maria at Christmas time, and the German Carols were ones we all loved to sing. The Spanish songs were often dances, and sometimes we tried to perform them as we sang.

These opportunities were very important to me because I loved singing despite the fact that I always frustrated my teachers by not being able to sing on pitch. I did not know I could not maintain pitch until I was in third or fourth grade, and after I learned the truth I found myself in the back row of every presentation, trying to blend my voice as best I could with the voices next to me. Luckily, my music teachers were all young women with wonderful energy, and with considerable talent both for music and for teaching. Most of them had a sense of humor that somehow managed to survive our questionable behavior. When I write "our," I mean we boys who, despite a love of song, managed to get into difficulties now and then that tried the patience of our lovely teachers.

Interestingly, I rarely told my parents much about what I was doing in school. They saw some of the homework I brought back from school, mainly in mathematics, sometimes in social studies, and they had an idea of what I was doing. Of course they knew my grades, which were undistinguished. But because of their own limited education they rarely could help me do any of my homework after the earliest grades. On the other hand, I never expected any help and was surprised when I discovered that some of my friends had parents who helped them with their work. I didn't think it was necessary. My point, though, is that while I could not always share much of what I was doing in school, I could easily share my experiences in my music classes. Often, I would sing the songs I learned so that everyone could enjoy them. I made a special point of regularly singing my songs to my grandmother Helena, as she lay in her sick-bed. It was a pleasure that she seemed to enjoy intensely, praising the song and singer both. One song that pleased her was "On the Road to Mandalay," which I sang with great vigor, and sometimes on pitch. Helena was an uncritical audience. I think she just loved the fact that she was not alone for the while that I could sing to her. In contrast, my grandmother Margaret rarely took an interest in song of any kind, and least of all in any songs I could sing.

Some Christmases stand out in my mind more than others. One of the oddest was when I was in second grade at the Sanford Street School. We rented the house at 45 Sanford Street, a very nice large house set back from the street. It had a fine front yard with two large maple trees symmetrically placed on each side of the walkway. The back yard was spacious, with an old outhouse that was no longer in use. Its working parts had been filled with gravel and stone, and I really did not know what it was for until long after we moved away. It seemed to me to be a simple small shed with some tools stored inside. Our house in Sanford Street was curious also for the fact that Mrs. Pearson and some of the people who lived with us as tenants in 22 Webster Place moved to our new house, so my parents were able to keep their finances on an even keel.

One of the most memorable of Christmases was spent at the Sanford Street house during one of those periods I remember from youth as having produced the most extreme snow storms. Indeed, there were many storms prior to Christmas itself, and outside the house the snow was piled high on both sides of the walk to the street and on both sides of the sidewalk for which we were responsible. That year I was able to shovel only a little bit before I got terribly sick. I had had chicken pox the year before, and this was measles, and it knocked me out for more than a week. I was dizzy, feverish, itchy, and grim. And it was coming up on Christmas.

When my teachers heard I was ill, they contacted my mother and brought some materials for me to work on while I was bedridden. There were two things I remember best. One was a cardboard replica of a watch face, with moveable arms. I could not yet tell time, despite my father's efforts using his own wrist watch. But slowly, I worked through with my mother the various quarter-to and quarter-after and half-past hours until I got the hang of it. Now it seems such a simple thing, but then it had stymied me.

The second thing my teacher provided me was a pack of cards with number problems that involved addition, subtraction, and I believe even multiplication and division. Again, these were exotic skills that I had not yet mastered in class, but it took only a short time for my mother to help me learn the mysteries involved in mathematical arts. What I remember so well is how patient my mother was and how encouraging my father was when he came home from work. My room was upstairs in the front of the house and stands in my mind as well lighted and fairly large. I must have been in bed in that room for the better part of three weeks, and in that time I was able to master tasks that had eluded me until then.

The year I was in bed for Christmas was surprising because my parents brought the Christmas tree up to my bedroom and set it up in front of one of the larger windows. That way the light from the street brightened the tree and made me very happy. My mother came in with decorations that almost hid the tree itself. There were no lights, but then we never had lights on our trees for fear of fire. But there were paper chains that I was able to make while sitting up in bed, and cut-out angels and stars and other designs that I was able to make that helped the tree glisten. Foil drippings were everywhere on the tree and on top was a red Santa hat. I don't think I was at the age when I still believed in Santa because I have a memory of my mother sitting on my bed and asking me about Santa. I told her I was waiting for Christmas, but not sure about Santa. She told me that she was thirteen before she realized that Santa was a wonderful myth, but not a real person. Today I find that remarkable.

To be sure I do not remember what my gifts were for Christmas, but I do remember that I could not give my parents anything more than Christmas Cards. But I meant all the sentiments that I was able to put in them. My uncle Richard was a very thoughtful man and came to see me a few times while I was sick. He owned an antique shop that we visited several times a month and this Christmas he gave me some interesting antiques. One was a regimental marching drum from a Union Army brigade. At that time I could not play drums at all – that came much later – but I remember the ornate paintings on the sides, all in Union colors of red, white, and blue, with a regimental eagle and crossed swords on one side and crossed rifles on the other. He also gave me a Union kepi and amazingly, a real Union rifle. I have no idea whether or not it could have been fired, but it never was while I had it. How my mother was convinced to let me have it I will never know.

When we moved back to 7 Webster Place our Christmases were a little more lavish, and I was fortunate enough to stay well and be able to participate entirely. Choosing the tree was always important, and one of the events I was able to take part in. I usually managed to get it set up in the dining room in the corner where my uncle Alfred sat. We moved his chair into another room, and he usually went to that room to sit. During the good years right after World War II, my father's customers showered him with gifts. Jewelers, designers, jewelry makers, and all those who bought precious metals from him were lavish when the war time austerity was over and people began again to buy their wares. Every day for weeks before Christmas, my father would come home from his office with packages of all kinds of gifts.

Sometimes he carried home three or four fifths of expensive whiskeys, Ballantines, Black and White, Cutty Sark, White Horse, and especially Haig & Haig Pinch, valued mainly for its nicely shaped bottle. Oddly, my father rarely ever drank, but he still felt it was important to have a good supply of scotch in the house. In addition to liquor, he would bring home fancy fruits from Oregon and the west coast, steaks from Omaha. Some of his customers actually made enough money from jewelry so that they could leave New York to buy and run fruit farms in the west, and some of those gifts were from those old friends. He was given huge assortments of chocolates from Switzerland or Holland, hundreds of cigars from Cuba, leather goods from the west, even silver-chased belts. The variety seemed unending. My father measured the state of the economy by the quality of his gifts.

On Christmas Eve in 1947 my father placed all that year's gifts under the tree or near it. He gave my mother three hundred dollars in one-dollar bills and placed them on the mantelpiece in the dining room. My mother crocheted two very large handbags, one brown and one black. Each handbag was made of "coins" of a heavy fabric that resembled the fabric in one of my lanyards. Each was strong, quite remarkable in appearance, and the bags that she created would have been a smash in the 1990s. The important thing to my mother was that she took several months for each bag, and as a point of pride she placed them under the tree.

That night we were robbed.

Snow had fallen steadily for a few days. Earlier that day I shoveled our driveway and the walkway by the side of the house as well as the broad steps to the porch and the front sidewalk. But I also watched as more snow filled in the driveway late that day. We were all in bed upstairs just after midnight. Without any of us sensing a thing, the robbers used a big-handled broad prying screwdriver to wedge open a cellar window and slide down into the half-full coal chute. The window was on the opposite side of the house from our bedrooms and the coal must have helped muffle their fall.

Their footprints and hand prints were coal black and prominent on the white door leading up from the basement to the first floor. They apparently felt their way through the house in the dark searching for anything they could easily take. It was also apparent when we found some of what they stole, that they must have made several sorties into the house and then back out to our car where they stashed the goods.

They took some of the presents, including boxes of cigars, some bottles of Scotch, some clothes, and my mother's handbags. They missed the currency stacked neatly on the mantelpiece, and missed the valuable silver in the breakfront in the foyer as they fled the house by the front door. They pushed our Model A through the snowy driveway and abandoned it down by Harrison Street because it wouldn't start. (Even my father had a hard time starting it in the dead of winter because he did not know how to use the choke.)   Because they got the

The foyer at 7 Webster Place

Model A out so far from the house, I think it is clear that they had help with them. I know from experience that in such deep snow as lay on the ground and in the driveway that year no single man could have moved the car unless he had figured out how to start it. And because that Model A made such a loud and distinctive noise when it ran, I do think one of us would have been awake while it drove down the driveway.

The chilly winter air roused my father thinking the coal furnace had gone out, but once down stairs he saw the front door standing wide open. He instantly knew we had been robbed and he called the police. He got dressed, woke us up, and we looked throughout the house. He found the window jimmied open in the cellar above the coal chute and I found the sturdy screwdriver the thief used. My father went out to search for the car and saw it not more than two hundred feet down the road, obstructing traffic. Relieved, he drove it back to the house, with some of the presents and his camel's hair coat stuffed inside. There was just too much Christmas bounty for the thieves to carry.

The police never caught the thieves, although they found some of the loot hidden in an old fashioned carriage barn behind a neighbor's house as if they expected to collect it later. This particular detail shows that the thieves had a plan and that they had ample time in our house to follow through on it. They must have come and gone from the house at least three times. We will never know. However, we knew that the year before the robbery we were called by a neighbor telling us there was a prowler on our porch while we were in the rear of the house listening to the radio. The police were called and discovered a Black man behind our garage and arrested him. We were told he was in prison for a year, so we assumed that he may have robbed us on this following Christmas Eve.

There was no question but that my mother was most distraught at the fact that the thief took the two handbags she had spent more than a year making. They were a labor of love and could have meant very little to the man who took them. Because I had watched her making these bags I knew just what they must have meant to her.

Today, of course, I am grateful that my father or mother did not wake up during the robbery and confront the burglars. I am also grateful that the robbers did not come upstairs and kill us all in our beds. It might have been a challenge because there were six of us, including my grandmothers, Helena and Margaret. My uncle Alfred was not home that night because he had found a sweetheart in New York State and was visiting her for the holidays.

Once the heat was on again and the house warm and the police finished with all their questions and some sense of normalcy returned, my parents did everything to make Christmas day seem as cheerful and joyous as we had hoped it would be. Our greatest gift was that none of us died on Christmas Eve.

A Threat of Murder and Another House Breaking

My father's brothers, in order oldest to youngest were Richard, Jack, then my father, Paul and Alfred. They were all people I really loved and enjoyed, except for my Uncle Jack, who had in his later years become a frightening man. Something happened to him that no one could ever understand. He changed from being a charming, witty, and thoughtful man to an alcoholic monster. My father blamed it on his wife, Jean, but he was wrong: she was a good woman. If we suffered because of Jack, then her suffering placed her in a realm some where near the early Christian Saints.

My earliest memories of Jack are good. His daughter, Jacqueline, was just a year or so younger than I, so we were able to play together when we were at 7 Webster Place. For a while he and his family, like ours, actually lived in the house and after they found their own place Jack was often there. He would visit his parents when we were not there.

He had a splashy tan Ford sedan, a 1936 model. We all went riding together to visit other relatives. One day I discovered in the back seat of that car, kneeling on the floor reading the Sunday comics, that I was given to car-sickness. I vomited all over his upholstery and had to get out of the car and wash myself off. Ever since, I have had to ride sitting straight up, watching the horizon, reading nothing. The smell of Jack's upholstery--before I vomited on it--brought on my illness. I have no idea what the fabric was, but in damp weather the odor would have made me ill even if the car were not moving.

He came to 7 Webster Place one Sunday afternoon when I was six and put two ice cream cones in the ice box. They were called Mello-Rolls, hard-frozen cylinders cut sharply at top and bottom and covered by a paper wrapper. The vanilla was especially creamy and vanilla-ish in ways that even the best ice cream today is not. This particular memory sticks in my mind because Jack eventually gave me and Jacqueline each one of the ice creams. I was given first choice and took the chocolate. Unfortunately that was the one Jacqueline wanted and she refused to eat the vanilla version. She cried and protested vigorously. In the course of the difficulty my Uncle Jack told her not to be jealous of what other people got. I didn't know what the word meant, but I figured it out, and ever after I unreasonably thought of Jacqueline as a jealous girl. Much later I discovered she became a generous and fulfilled woman who seemed undestroyed by the early calamities of life.

My earliest memories of Uncle Jack are all good. He was smart, quick, and a good talker. He also dressed with considerable style, especially his shoes, two-tone and snappy, with brown silk socks and black clocks. He wore felt hats with panache and loved his Ford car, which was newer than our old chalky-blue/gray roadster.

Like his older brothers, he was too old for the army when war broke out. But he did not thrive in the economic upturn of the early 1940s even though he found work in something related to the war effort at the Pickatinny Arsenal in Rockaway Township. The arsenal dated to before the Civil War and was put into service as war began to threaten. The work paid a fair wage and he must have done it well enough. I saw photographs of him in a handsome work uniform with other well dressed and cheerful men. In the early years he was never in need and his family seemed happy. But some time in 1944 or so Jack began drinking and never stopped. And when he drank he became a vicious and mean man. His family must have suffered from his brutality, but my cousin Jacqueline never said a word about those years to me.

He lost his job soon enough when he began drinking. And at the same time he had one of his first epileptic fits. He seems to have grown into epilepsy the way some people grow out of it. His fits were frightening and like a natural disaster, like a tornado, with Jack writhing and uttering guttural sounds and thrashing on the ground. It is possible, we thought, that they were somehow "produced" by his heavy drinking. He was never examined carefully enough for anyone to know much about it. He had no regular doctor and was medicated strictly from the Emergency Room of the Orange Memorial Hospital. By that time he was impoverished and living on welfare in a dark, dismal, floor-through in Orange in a painful neighborhood.

My father's reaction was typical. He helped Jack's family. He went to visit Jack and often gave aunt Jean money for food. There was never any food in the house when my father and I went to visit. Much of the time Jack himself would be out somewhere drinking, but it also seems that he was such a problem that even the local taverns would not let him in. He made a point of hiding liquor bottles throughout his apartment. Aunt Jean one day told my father that in his absence she had gone through the house, found bottles and had thrown the contents down the sink. She also told us that Welfare paid the rent for them so that they would never be evicted--which is what would have happened if the money had been given directly to Jack. Sometimes my father gave aunt Jean ten dollars for herself, then handed her another ten to give up to Jack when he came back and found out my father had been there. Otherwise Jack would have forced her to give all the money over to him.

It still seems astounding to me that my father could have given Jack's family as much as he did, since we ourselves had relatively little. My father's income, $25 a week, was low through those years, but it was steady, and my father did not drink or waste his money. He saved what he could, which was almost nothing, and made a little on the side when he could manage the estate sales. So he had something that he could give to aunt Jean to help the family survive. He gave it without begrudging it. Uncle Richard and Uncle Paul also gave Jack money and help when they could, but nothing any of the brothers did could affect his behavior.

In the late 1940s Jack was in bad shape. Sometimes he came to our house looking for a handout from my father. He had a hard time remembering that my father worked and that he would not be there on a weekday afternoon. Once when I was about ten he showed up in the back driveway as I was shooting baskets into the hoop attached to the front of the garage. He stood there watching me, his hands in his pockets, wearing an old shirt and baggy pants that showed his white socks and dusty shoes. He was scrawny, chicken-necked, reddened in the sun and forlorn looking. The ball bounced off the rim and he retrieved it and in a nice motion using both hands he sunk a set shot from about fifteen feet. I was impressed. I shot a basket then passed the ball to him and he shot another. For a period of about six minutes our friendship was cemented by a game.

He asked me if my parents were home, and I told him no. His mother Helena was upstairs in bed and he told me that he would go in and visit. I stayed outside and shot a few more baskets, but eventually I got tired chasing the bouncing ball and decided to go into the house. I found Jack in the pantry. He knew where my father kept the Haig & Haig and he had gone right to it instead of going upstairs to visit Helena. He was there with a glass of Scotch in his hand and the bottle on the counter in front of him. He looked at me for a moment, then said, "You won't tell on me, will you?" I resented him for this. I understood the effects of liquor primarily because of my watching his drunkenness. Yet he pulled the school ground trick of pledging me to secrecy as if we were somehow bound together by a brief session of basketball in the backyard.

Fortunately, he left the house soon enough. He was not drunk then, only drinking. We were very uneasy with each other. I feared him because of his tendency to violence and he feared me because I knew something he did not want me to know. We spoke almost not at all. I watched him closely until he finally left. I watched him out of fear.

Months later he came to the house on a Sunday when we were all home. His pretense was a visit to his mother, which seemed natural enough even though these days he rarely visited. We were downstairs after our Sunday dinner and my father went up to talk to him. Jack was very distraught and came downstairs raving about the house and his dead father. My father was soon after him trying to calm him down. We had not realized when he first came how drunk he was, but it was now clear that he was beyond help.

He shouted and said, "I'm going to kill you all." He whirled around and began back up the stairs when my father tried to grab him. Jack was wiry and very powerful, especially when he was drinking and fearless. He broke free and went up the stairs screaming that he would get his father's gun and kill us. He knew my grandfather's Colt naval revolver was in the locked cabinet in the hallway. He reached it first and tried to pull the doors open. They held firm. He then went looking for something to pry the doors open with and my father grabbed him. I had come up the stairs myself and tackled Uncle Jack to push him away from the doors. He screamed and smashed at both of us while my mother shouted up from the downstairs. She was going to call the police.

After a struggle, we got Jack back downstairs and the police were never called. But he was furious and out of control and stomped out on the porch and threatened never to come back, accusing my father of stealing the house and not taking care of their mother. Jack was irrational and in pain and he got away from the house and went home. It was a terrifying experience for us. That very day my father got the gun out of the cabinet and began the process of getting rid of it permanently. It was obviously more threatening to us than it ever would be to anyone outside the family.

Only two years after that incident, and after Helena died, my mother, father, and I went out to the Hollywood theater to see a Bette Davis film on a Saturday night. It was an event when all of us were able to go together to see a movie and we strolled back slowly on a summer's evening with the darkness only just having settled in. We never left any lights on in the house when we went out, so when we got on the porch and my father opened the door, I went into the living room to turn on the nearest lamp. But as I did so, I tripped over something. And when I got the light on I screamed. A body was stretched on the floor of the living room face down. I had no idea what or who it was, but my father realized at once that it was my Uncle Jack.

He was passed out on the living room floor either from drink or from an epileptic seizure. An ambulance took him to Orange Memorial Hospital, but he did not regain consciousness until the next morning. How he got in the house was a mystery until we went to the kitchen and found that he had broken the window over the kitchen sink and climbed through. Then we saw that he had cut himself and had dripped blood throughout the house.

But we also saw that he had gotten into the liquor cabinet and had taken enough to keep him drunk for a week. That was all he wanted, although we feared he may have also been bent on violence against us. We never learned what he was up to. But that evening was one of the most terrifying that I remember at the house.

We moved a year or two later, in 1951, and that ended Jack's haunting 7 Webster Place. At first my father did not give him our new address, but he soon found us in the telephone book. My father continued visiting aunt Jean and his family, Jacqueline, Patty, and later Johnny, but we never saw Uncle Jack in our house again. Eventually, Uncle Jack figured out my father's commuting schedule and would show up at the train station around 6:30 or 7:00 in the evening and beg for handouts. My father would give him a few dollars because he knew if he gave him more he would get even more drunk. By that time Uncle Jack was a wiry wreck of a man speaking in a vicious rasp.

My father must have been horribly embarrassed to see him waiting for him at the train station, but he never said anything about that. What he did talk about was the pain of seeing his brother in such a terrifying condition. I remember once telling my father that I would have liked to have had a twin and he tried to explain to me that it might not have been an unmixed blessing.

Jack stabilized himself as a functioning alcoholic, but not of the country club variety. Or rather, of the country club variety, but outside the pale of membership. He became a golf caddy at a local public golf course. He could have had no regular employment there, none sanctioned by the course overseers. So he must have hung around the club house and offered his services to likely golfers. He made money almost every day during the golf season. But he had to endure the winters with no work. Uncle Jack was rarely sick, and never sober for all the rest of his life. He muddled through his days as best he could. Aunt Jean grew old and pained looking and stayed with him even though she did not drink herself. She was old beyond her years when I last saw her.

The violence stopped but the drinking never did. Uncle Jack would have been a remarkable advertisement for the virtues of Alcoholics Anonymous and the horrors of drink, not that any drunk would know enough to pay attention. I often wonder why nobody had ever thought to do anything about Uncle Jack's drinking except complain. No one ever suggested that he see a counselor or a doctor or a psychiatrist. It was a thing not done in those years. There may have been no one at that time who could have helped. Alcoholics Anonymous was only a little more than 10 years old, and I never heard anyone mention its name.

Uncle Jack died suddenly and unexpectedly in his seventies. It seems to have been heart failure, but there were other complications brought on by drink, under-nourishment, and exhaustion. His wife lived ten or more years after him and was moved into newly constructed public supported senior-citizen living quarters where she and her son Johnny lived together. She said she was very happy in the new apartments, which must certainly have been like heaven in comparison with the dark hole in which she had spent most of her life. I am especially glad that she felt she had a few happy years at the end of her life because she paid a terrible price to be married to Uncle Jack. At least two of his children grew up and moved away to live successful and happy lives. Both were dedicated to their mother. The third child, Johnny, stayed with her. He never worked at a sustaining job but lived with a mysterious disability and died very soon after his mother.

Thinking of Uncle Jack now, I wish we had been able to understand what demons drove him and I wish we could have helped him. He tried to take us all with him on his painful journey, but he couldn't. He traveled alone, tortured to the end.

The House Becomes a Hospice

Margaret Byrne, my mother's mother, was a huge woman, perhaps five foot five, with a fifty-five inch waist. She wore large white whalebone corsets that imparted a strange, upholstered look. She liked pink and green flowered house-dresses of the kind one found in department stores or in the Sears and Roebuck catalog. She wore sturdy shoes, no makeup, no jewelry, and a flat top hat, usually straw or felt. Her hair was white, full, and wavy. She parted it in the middle and wore a stout bun at the back of her head. Her photographs reveal a powerful-looking woman with, in her last years, a slightly masculine face.

One photograph shows Margaret standing in an alleyway with her sister Jane next to her. The two of them, proportioned identically, make a prepossessing duo. My mother many years later gave me the photograph, taken with a Kodak box camera in the mid forties, and asked me to re-photograph it and remove Jane from the picture entirely. I studied the photograph for a while and commented to myself on its Diane Arbus qualities. I told my mother that I would have been proud to have taken that photograph--a comment that totally baffled her. Then I realized that indeed I *had* taken the photograph one day when I was about twelve when they took me to the cement alleyway and memorialized Margaret's visit to Jane's home.

Margaret had a difficult life. She came from a comfortable Irish Catholic family, the Hughes's, which had early risen into respectability. She had been a dutiful girl, going to Catholic schools, and performing her religious duties as she was

Margaret Byrne and her sister Jane Schoener

being a nun, teaching school, or enjoying the missionary life in Asia or Africa. But her duties were odious. She cleaned chamber pots, prepared the nuns' laundry, worked in the kitchen, and finally scrubbed the entryway stairs and floor. It was while she was on her hands and knees on the floor with soap and brush that a nun entered and abused her so brutally that she quit. She backed out and found herself in limbo, with no calling, and no prospects.

Around this time she met her future husband, Edward Byrne. He was a tall, large man, with a powerful build and a direct rough manner. He was a ship builder and steam fitter born in Liverpool after his parents had emigrated from Ireland. They were poor people, but they had somehow ended up in Bloomfield, New Jersey, before the turn of the century. Margaret and Edward married and life was comfortable and interesting by virtue of the sociability of both their families. Edward's family was successful in America and they seemed to have been cheerful and plentiful. Margaret's family may have been a touch more gracious and socially charming. Margaret's uncle Martin was a smart business man and always had a good word for her. Theirs was a song-filled household with jolly and prosperous relatives who knew how to have a good time.

Tragedy struck Margaret early on. My mother was the first born, then came my Uncle Billy, my Uncle Robbie, and while Margaret was pregnant with my Uncle Eddy, her husband died suddenly of pneumonia. She was shattered. She had no skills, no education, and no work experience. She also had very little money and no obvious way of making more. Her prospects, with a nine year old daughter and three other children, were frightening at best. Her family helped her at first, but they could not support her and her family indefinitely. So she did the only thing she could think of. She took in laundry. That meant that she had to go to families who were better off than their neighbors and ask for work. She went to their homes, gathered their laundry, brought it to her home, did the laundry by hand, dried it, ironed it, folded it, and then returned it. All for very few dollars a load. My mother helped her by managing the boys, especially Eddy the newborn. She also helped with the laundry itself. It is no surprise that my mother Julia married as early as she could in order to get out of her household. It was deprived of joy and comfort. And her brothers made her life miserable. They were uncouth, difficult, and bold.

All this took place with Margaret living in various tenements in Bloomfield and Orange, rows of attached buildings strung on for sometimes an entire city block. Each would have its own entry stairs--a stoop--with a pointed roof covering them, and each entry would let in at least two, sometimes four families. The back porches supported clotheslines strung out to the nearest telephone poles. There was nothing convenient in this situation for Margaret and her work. She had been a beautiful young woman before she married, but she soon grew coarse-looking and defeated by her regimen of gathering and doing the laundry.

I saw one of the tenements in Bloomfield where my mother lived as a young woman. It was drab, but clean and neat. At the time I had no sense of its meaning, nor of the implications of tenement living: an environment in which everyone knew your business and in which every slight distinction from your neighbors was a signal for envy and jealousy. The wooden buildings presented a row of identical facades, plain and to my eyes quite innocent. They had a special meaning to my mother, and she stood looking at them for a long time when we visited.

After her laundering days were done, Margaret lived on her own with her son Eddy for a short while, although I do not know how she supported herself. When she needed help she began living with us in the late 1930s. She was fifty-five years old at the time. She took on some of the daily chores in the kitchen when we lived at 22 Webster Place. She may have done other things as well, although I do not recall her cleaning or vacuuming. However, she did her own laundry and hung the sheets and other laundry on the clothes-line stretched diagonally from the back of the house.

As a child I never considered her happiness, just as I never thought about the happiness of anyone, including myself. I do not recall any of us asking whether anyone else was happy or not. That seemed an unnecessary question. My grandmother does not, in retrospect, seem to have been happy living with us. She had a small allowance or pension--possibly connected with her husband's death, but beyond that nothing. She had no car--everyone used the bus in those days--and therefore she had very little independence despite being a fiercely independent woman. When she couldn't do what she wanted to do, she became frustrated and annoyed. Beyond her sense of having been put upon, she undoubtedly resented living with her daughter and her husband. I never heard them having words, but they had a clear hierarchical relationship with my mother on top. There were times when my grandmother would shush me because Julia was not in a good mood. She never took these times lightly nor did she pretend amusement at my mother's occasional archness. The problems that Margaret faced were the same that any woman living in another woman's household would face: the loss of authority and the expectation of doing as she was told.

When Margaret lived with us at 22 Webster Place she had the bedroom on the first floor in the front of the house. I had a bedroom at the back of the first floor in what was originally a dining room. Margaret in that house was angry and distant much of the time, although I was very young then and remember her best from age six, when I was generally in her care. Her method of caring for me was to wait for my parents to leave for work, then shove me out the side door and tell me to play until lunch time. After a brief lunch, a glass of milk and either a ketchup or mayonnaise sandwich (my favorite), I would then be shunted outside again until shortly before my mother returned home. It didn't matter how hot it was or how cold it was. And since there were no other children my age on that side of the street, I always played alone. Many's the time that I banged loudly on the door to try to come inside when it was winter, but Margaret never opened the door. I was locked out.

There were many times at 22 Webster Place when I was not a good boy. God only knows how serious my infractions were when I was five and six years old, but they were serious. My punishment was to go out into the back yard to the privet hedge and cut myself a "switch," which was a stout stick about three feet long and a half inch or so in diameter. When I had done that I had to bring it into the house and then my grandmother would beat me on the tush or on the legs with it until I learned my lesson. She did this often enough so that I have extremely vivid memories of the events. Among the possible bad deeds I could have committed I can think of only a few: writing with chalk on a neighbor's sidewalk, for which I was duly disciplined; traversing the bounds and going into a neighbor's backyard, ditto; "borrowing" a toy from a neighbor's backyard, ditto; crying at an inappropriate time, ditto.

Margaret had few pleasures partly because she had little or no money and little time in which to spend it. When she did get a few dollars and wanted to go "downtown" to see the stores she never took me. I sometimes watched her striding purposely down the street pleased with herself on her way to an afternoon matinee at the Palace or the Hollywood Theater. She strolled down Harrison Street, much fancier than Webster Place with its large apartment buildings and numerous small shops, and seemed to be presenting herself to the neighborhood.

She did not have personal occupations, such as my mother did. She read very little if at all. She did not sew, except to mend a garment, and she did not knit. She cooked terribly and only as often as strictly necessary. When I think about it, I cannot remember her doing anything especially creative to occupy her time. She did some laundry, of course, and she spent time sorting and storing her clothing. And she did do some ironing while listening to the radio, which she did during the day in much the same way people now watch daytime television.

During the Depression, hoboes stopped at our house at lunchtime and sometimes at dinner time. My grandmother would greet them--very coldly--at the side door of the house. Usually at meal times I would be inside having my own meal and when a hobo came to the door it was my responsibility to deal with him. Margaret would tell me a hobo was here and I would go and talk to him. Usually they were men in their thirties and forties, bedraggled, dirty, ashamed. They were sometimes white men and sometimes Black men. It made no difference to us. They would ask for something to eat. I would then leap into action. "Do you want a ketchup sandwich or a mayonnaise sandwich?" I would ask them. I then gave them a sandwich in wax paper. Margaret and I sometimes went to the front of the house and watched them as they walked away enjoying their trophy.

We knew the Depression was over some time in late 1941 when I made a hobo a ketchup sandwich, slathering the ketchup on thickly as I could. I wrapped it in wax paper, gave it to him, and he thanked me. I also gave him a glass of water, which he drank right there--then returned the glass. We went to the front of the house, watched him, and only a few steps down the road he opened the sandwich, took a bite, and after a moment's hesitation threw it into the street. "No more," my grandmother said. "No more sandwiches for any of them. If they're too good for our sandwiches we will eat them ourselves. No more sandwiches for any of the buggers." And she kept to that decision. We never gave another hobo another bite of anything. The Depression was over.

Margaret moved across the street with us to number 7 after a brief series of moves through East Orange. My parents sold 22 Webster Place in 1943 to rent a house on Carnegie Place near Nassau School, where I was in second grade.That was a very small second-floor-through apartment with very little space. My grandmother was there with us and had her own room. My room was just off the living room, and part of that year I spent in bed with a variety of normal childhood illnesses, the worst of which was chicken pox. While in that house I was the subject

Nassau Elementary School,
now Ecole Toussaint Louverture

of a "situation." The little girl up the street, also about seven, and I were discovered taking off each other's clothes. A phone call informed my grandmother and she astounded me with her understanding. I did not get switched, and she agreed that if I did not do it again the story would go no further. My parents would not be involved. Amazing. She assumed I'd been lured into this lewd behavior by the girl, which was only partly true.

We lived in that house for almost a year, then rented 45 Sanford Street where I transferred to a new school for third grade. My grandmother was with us in that house and took up her usual duties. After that year, we moved back to 7 Webster Place, where we stayed for the next seven years. Margaret was usually found sitting in one of the brown comfortable soft chairs in the dining room listening to the radio, or else out on one of the rocking chairs on the porch watching the passing parade, as she called it.

In the evenings after dinner her favorite pastime was to go across the street to visit with Mrs. Breitenbach and her boarders. Many of the houses on Webster Place took in boarders at that time. The Breitenbach house was number 16, a very large house painted a lemon yellow, with a wide porch that spanned not only the front of the house, but turned the corner on each side, so there was a great deal of sitting room. It was covered in places by rambling roses that I admired as a child. Mrs. B, as we called her, and some of her regulars sat out on their porch of an evening, listening to the cicadas in the summer, swatting mosquitoes, marveling at the fireflies. The long hot summer evenings in those years were much richer with insect life than they are today. Margaret would come home pleased with life from her talks with Mrs. B. She would know all about the neighborhood gossip. She would know who was moving out, who wasn't talking to whom, and what everyone thought of everyone else's house. Nothing was missed on those excursions.

It was after one of them, around 8:30 on a summer evening, that I saw Margaret being led back to our house by Mrs. B. and a friend. Margaret had a shocked look on her face. Her mouth hung open, her eyes were wide and unrecognizing, her arms were held up on each side by the women who steered her carefully up the stairs of the porch. We had no idea what was wrong. I called for my mother the minute I saw grandma and she came quickly, hearing the fear in my voice. We each took an arm and while moving her forward tried to talk to her. But she could not understand us and she could not talk. Her tongue seemed to loll strangely in her mouth as if she could not control it. Fortunately she could walk, and fortunately we were able to get her upstairs. If she could not have walked we certainly could not have lifted her.

My mother described the symptoms over the phone and the doctor knew it was serious. He arrived when Margaret was lying rigidly on the bed, apparently asleep. He took out his blood pressure sleeve, checked her numbers, then checked her temperature and felt her temples. He looked at her eyes with a speculum and opened her mouth. "She's had a stroke," he said. "A serious one." He left us in mortal fear that Margaret might die before the morning, but that was not the case. Both my father and mother were tense with anxiety. My father trained during the war as a medical assistant in case of bombing in New York, but his training did not consider the possibility of stroke.

My father's mother Helena lay in the next room in bed dying of cancer—so in one terrifying instant the house had become a hospice.

I had no idea what a stroke was. Mrs. B. came to the house the next morning and told my mother that Margaret was talking quite well one moment, then suddenly shouted and grabbed at her head and then started jabbering, making sounds no one could understand. Mrs. B. said she knew it was a stroke the minute it happened, but that kind of claim was typical of Mrs. B. and other neighbors as well. She went up to talk to Margaret, but all she got was the distant, confused stare that was typical of her at the time. She seemed not to know anyone was there.

We took food up to her, soup and tea. My mother tried to feed Margaret, but it was not possible at first, and then when it became possible it was not easy. Margaret could be gotten into an upright sitting position only with real effort on our part. Then she did not seem to understand what we wanted her to do with the spoon. Next, we found that she could not control the muscles of her lips and much of the soup dribbled out of the side of her mouth. We fed her on one side and mopped up after her on the other for many days. I have no memory of how my mother dealt with the bedpan, although I recall carrying it down the hall to the bathroom myself, then washing it out carefully before returning it.

I was puzzled by all that went on. I often hung outside Margaret's room readying myself for action, although I had no idea what kind of action it might be. I helped my mother move her in the bed, fix the bedclothes, and try to communicate. After a week or so Margaret began to understand us and made signals when she understood what we said. My mother told her that she had a stroke but that the doctor said she might mend well if she stayed in bed and got enough rest. I recall--or think I recall--that Margaret was able sometimes to get up and go to the bathroom on her own, but that was much later, when she began to understand her situation.

After two months she started to talk again, although it was all but impossible to understand her at first. Her lips could not form the shapes she needed in order express her words, so it frustrated everyone. It took close on to a year for her to get up and around again and be understood. There were many things she could not do at all, including anything that required close finger dexterity. I tied her shoe laces, buttoned dresses, and dealt with detail work, such as threading needles for her mending. Eventually I was called on to support her when she started to walk again. She wanted to go downstairs, to go out on the porch, to get to see the world. I did what I could to help her. I sat with her on the porch, answered her questions, and was generally dismayed to see how little of herself seemed to remain with her.

Two years later, she had still recovered only partially. She could walk, she could understand what they said on the radio, and she could communicate, although with difficulty. She was not in a wonderful frame of mind during this period, and if it had not been for her having a powerful drive and a difficult personality, she might not have recovered as much as she did.

She died suddenly. Without much warning. She had a gall bladder attack late at night and was transferred to a Catholic hospital in Newark. She was more worried about whether her underwear was clean than how sick she was. But everyone in the family knew that a hospital stay meant that one would probably not survive to see one's home ever again. And that was the case with Margaret. She was operated upon and died from complications of the operation on August 24, 1949. What these complications might have been, I do not know. However, I remember the surgeon talking about trying to get through the layers of fat to remove the gangrenous gall bladder and that he could do nothing to save her.

Her sons were present at the wake and wondered if there was any money to be left to them. Apparently, Margaret had inherited $1500 from a brother who died in Los Angeles and had been involved in the founding of the family-named chain of drug stores, the Hughes chain. According to my sister Doris, Margaret gave $500 of her inheritance to my mother, but kept the rest of the money for her own use to finance her movies, her excursions, and her occasional treats. Some of this money had been distributed, although in odd ways. My mother had a seal coat of Margaret's redone for herself. She also bought several expensive suits from an upscale store named Doops. And she bought a coat from Margaret's sister, Jane, for $20 to give to Doris. At the wake, my father gave Margaret's bank book to Doris for reasons that baffled her. She did not look at it, but simply said, "This has nothing to do with me," and gave it back to him.

It was my father's responsibility to bury--and pay for burying--most of the people in the family. If Margaret had any money left, which I doubt, it went to the funeral home. Margaret's sons did not get an inheritance and I think they suspected that there was money they should have gotten. Since no one had any money to start with, and since her sons never gave her more than $20 now and then, money was important when she died. I remember my uncles being very agitated, and more than once I thought there might have been a scuffle in the living room at 7 Webster Place. Somehow, however, things were held together and serious arguments avoided. We buried Margaret in the Catholic cemetery and, since Helena died less than a year before, that was the end of the hospice era. My mother experienced menopause at this time and suffered an emotional collapse. I have seen entries in her Missal from this year and realize that she was in a state of crisis for many months and even years. One touching passage she typed out on the back of a *Judy's Silver Shop* invoice is:

Lord, I am now in tribulation, and my heart is not at ease: but I am much afflicted with my present suffering. Give me patience, Help me, O my God and I will not fear, how much soever I may be distressed. Thine almighty hand is able to take away from me this temptation also, and to moderate its violence, as you have often done heretofore for me, O my

She often told me how difficult this period in her life was, and even though I was there throughout, I realize it was much more trying than I could have understood as a young person. From the perspective of an adult, I see now what an impossible task my parents had been handed, and especially how trying it had been for my mother. Every calamity ate away at the independence and freedom of everyone in the house. It is easy now to see why taking refuge in the spiritual reassurances of a Missal helped people through the day.

My Sister Was an Only Child

My big sister always delighted me. In the late 1930s we all lived together for a short while in 7 Webster Place, but I do not associate that house with her. Instead, I remember her when I was four, five, and six living in the house across the street, 22 Webster Place. I remember so well the afternoons we danced together to Glenn Miller tunes on the third floor, which was her private suite. We had an old radio up by the front window and we listened to "String of Pearls," "Tuxedo Junction," 'Honeysuckle Rose," "American Parade," "Blues in the Night," and "Sing, Sing, Sing," on WNEW, "The Milkman's Matinee," a program of swing tunes designed for dancing, although not quite anticipating a foxtrotting seventeen year-old girl and a stumbling five year-old boy. But I loved it, and Doris enjoyed it too.

My sister Doris was in many ways an unlucky girl. She would tell you that much. She blamed her parents for divorcing at a time when people simply did not divorce. Surely, it ruined her childhood. She, like Julia, lost a father at an early age. Her grandmother Westlake was a wonderful woman whom I met only once, not having the faintest idea who she was or what her relation to my mother was. My mother and I took a long hot bus ride to Belleville to visit Mrs. Westlake one hot summer afternoon when I was eight. She was a lovely, large, gentle woman. We sat on a dark shaded screened in porch and talked. She asked me, "Do you have a wheel?" But I did not know that a "wheel" was a bicycle and I could not answer her. The answer would have been "no," although I had still had a tricycle that I had outgrown.

Grandmother Westlake was a fine woman and she looked after Doris for a while when she was young, around the time my mother was mending from her car accident. Curiously, when we speak about her, Doris always refers to Julia as "*My* mother," and when I refer to her it is also as "*My* mother." I asked Doris about this anomaly one day and she had no clue as to why we used that locution when we should have been saying, "*Our* mother." I realize now that it has to do with the fact that Doris had Julia as her mother all to herself (even when they were separated) for twelve years, then I had Julia to myself from age six—my age at which Doris married--and onward. We both regarded ourselves as only children, and our subconscious awareness of that fact comes out in our referring to Julia as *my* mother, something we continued until Doris died.

In some essential fashion Doris felt unloved. Her father, Tom, was pleasant enough in many ways, but he did not adopt Doris as his own in any sense. He seems to have been distant and often was not home at the Westlakes when she was there. When Doris was able to visit back and forth on her own, her father had a girlfriend and he often spent time with her. She was known, not necessarily affectionately, as "The Polack." I know nothing about her other than that she took Tom's affections and

My sister Doris at 15

made Doris feel all the more unwanted.

On the other hand, Doris loved her grandmother Westlake. She lived in Belleville and had a house with people who had a great sense of joy. Doris talks about the liveliness of the household and how much fun she had with her cousins. The house was not just a house. It was also a business. The downstairs was a newspaper shop and people would come up on the porch and into the main room where they could buy magazines, papers, and sundries. It was one of the reasons that the house was so lively. However, when I went to visit, all traces of the shop were gone. Times had changed.

Doris was educated in Catholic schools and seems to have enjoyed her studies. She was an excellent student, having decided early on that she wanted to be a nurse. One of the consequences of her being enrolled in Our Lady Help of Christians school and of living with my parents was that Julia enrolled her as Doris Jacobus rather than as Doris Westlake. Again, the reasons were in order to respect appearances, something that in most ways dominated my mother's approach to life. She did not want to admit to the authorities at Doris's school that she was divorced. But when Tom Westlake saw Doris's school report card and realized Julia had changed her name, however informally, he became seriously put out. "So, she's gone and changed your name, has she? No more Westlake is it? Well, by God that's the end of it then." And he apparently turned his back on her and left Doris completely on her own.

Unlike most of the rest of the family, Doris got to high school, but she also decided to leave school a month before graduation to get married. That resulted in her postponing her ambitions for almost thirty years. Years later, with considerable difficulty, and against substantial odds, Doris got her college degree and became a nurse after all. But again, nothing for Doris came easily. She had to work hard and deal with people close to her who would have been just as happy to see her denied the rewards that she knew were rightfully hers. She got what she had by grit and determination.

I have talked with her about her early years, but her stories are convoluted and difficult to understand--at least for me. I am vague about a number of important things. I realize from what she says that she spent a long time with each of her grandmothers. Margaret, Julia's mother, was very close to Doris and when she speaks of Margaret, Doris is very appreciative and positive in her memories. My memories of Margaret--Grandma--are not the same. But Doris seems to have been "left off" at least for a while at Margaret's when she was very little. Julia had to work, so Doris was often taken care of by Margaret. Then there was a period of time when Doris was shunted off to her Grandmother Westlake for extended visits.

Doris was always angry at her mother for having left her in the care of others so much of the time. I'm not sure what choices our mother had, but Doris saw her so differently that her picture of our mother is of a woman who lolled in bed until late in the morning, who spent most of her time on herself rather than on Doris, and who enjoyed considerable personal indulgence throughout her life. Doris also saw her as a woman who aspired to be better than others, to affect a superior pose. Doris was certainly right in assuming that Julia was concerned with appearances and that she was anxious to appear to belong to something other than the poor Irish laundering class into

Doris at 12, with Helena, Julia, and Ernest
on the Boardwalk at Atlantic City

which she was born. I regard her efforts as part of her hope of bettering herself and I never saw the qualities of self indulgence that Doris saw--or at least I will say I did not see them expressed in anything of the sort Doris may have seen.

Ironically, at age twelve or thirteen, Doris was also in an automobile accident. However, she was not in a car–she was hit by a car. On a difficult corner in East Orange, off Park Avenue where Best & Co. used to be, she stepped off the curb coming home from Our Lady Help of Christians school, and was hit by a car. Her back was injured and a long period of recovery was involved. There was also a lawsuit involved, and the family lawyer, Dick Spitz, represented Doris and secured a settlement. How the money was involved, I really do not know. Doris certainly got very little from it, essentially nothing more than a "fake camel's hair coat," as she once told me. Doris thought that her mother had spent most of the money herself, although some must have been used for living expenses.

When I was in my first year of high school many years later, I saw an educational film about traffic safety in which a young girl was shown stepping off the very curb that Doris had stepped from and being hit by a passing car. I do not know if the film was inspired by Doris's accident, but it certainly looked as if it were.

When my parents got married in 1933 Doris was almost ten. They lived at first in 7 Webster Place, and Doris left her grandmother to move in with her mother and my father. The marriage was not a happy event for Doris, who must have seen it as a final impediment to her own parents getting back together. There was never any question of that happening, but for children of divorced parents, the fantasy of reconciliation and a return to "normal" relations is always operative, whether consciously or unconsciously.

The marriage made Doris feel homeless and unwanted.

Soon, however, my father insisted that Doris needed to be with the new family, so she lived with us in 7 Webster Place while my grandparents were still alive. This arrangement was shortlived until we all moved across the street to 22 Webster Place, where she had the top floor all to herself. And despite her feelings of rejection, which persisted even after she moved in with us, she always treated me with great affection and tenderness. She dressed me and took care of me and taught me to dance at an early age, and when she had her first boyfriend she taught me something about romance as well.

Doris seemed happy enough when living at 22 Webster Place. She had her own space and she never complained, at least to me. If she misbehaved and was disciplined I was somewhere out of the picture at such times. I saw her once having been in great pain with ear trouble. At the time no one would have thought to call a doctor about such things, but everyone seemed to have a home remedy that had been passed down from the elders. In this case I remember distinctly seeing her from a distance in her room, sitting on a chair with several women around her (not my mother however) while our Aunt Betty Byrne poured some warm oil or other liquid from the lid of a jar into her ear. It produced agonizing screams from Doris and I am rather surprised, given the level of pain, that it did not produce deafness as well. I watched all of this from a distance, standing outside the large room in which all this took place. It has a surreal quality to it now as I re-envision the scene.

Some time before the war, Doris got herself an after school job. She went to work for the Kress Company in its large, wonderful five and ten cent store on Central Avenue. It was a general all purpose store with amazingly high ceilings, hanging lights, and counter after counter of goods. Off to one side was the luncheon counter where I often went with my mother to get BLTs and ice cream sodas. On the other side of the huge open space was the candy counter. That was where Doris worked, keeping the candy bins filled, selling various assortments from the large, attractive displays. It was a good job, but she did not last long because she wound up eating the profits. I'm not sure how or why she decided the leave that job, but she soon parted ways with Kress and Co.

When I was four and five, Doris had a steady boyfriend. He was a young man, bright, very upbeat and cheerful. He knew how to tumble with me and how to make me feel important even when I wasn't. Howard Cullen was a family favorite. Doris thought he was wonderful and Julia agreed. Howard had a talent for getting along with young and old alike. The fact that he charmed me and Julia both--not to mention Doris--meant only that he had social skills that are rare at any age.

He was also good looking and athletic. He moved with ease, threw the ball with ease, and seemed very comfortable in his body. He and Doris had a great deal of fun. They listened to big band music and they lolled in the sun together. We had a small backyard at 22 Webster Place always thick with grass. Usually the wash line was up and often there was wash hanging outside. But I recall several days in the summer when Cullen, as everyone called him, came to visit and went out in the backyard and simply stretched on the grass with Doris and me and talked the afternoon out. I felt comfortable with them and I loved being there in the grass even though the ants walked across my face and arms and the sun was red through my squnched eyelids. They tried to get me to nap, but I stayed fiercely awake, anxious not to miss a word.

Doris and Howard were very serious and seemed likely to marry, but the world interfered. Cullen went into the army in early 1942 and was gone. He may have wanted to marry before he left and my parents may have said no. Nothing has been said about that. But it is clear that marriage was on Doris's mind as her only way of getting out of the house.

With Cullen away and the war on she probably had no

clear sense of what her options were. She met Paul DiLeo through a girlfriend and began to see him at first without her parents knowing. Paul was a cheerful, self-confident young man with a car. He had been in the Marines before the war but was discharged for something that left him 4-F, unfit for military service. Therefore, he was available and represented her best chance for marriage.

My parents did not take to him. He was not like Cullen. He did not make a special effort to charm the parents, although he was in no way hostile or rude. He simply did not have the personal charm that made Cullen such a special person. I have a much dimmer memory of him before Doris married him than I do of Cullen. He spent less time with me, and I was obviously of little importance to him. He and Doris decided to get married before Doris finished high school. Paul himself had not finished high school and he did not think this an impediment. Our mother was heartbroken at this news and tried everything to get Doris to change her mind, but nothing worked.

Apart from the fact that my mother felt Doris ruined her chances in life by not graduating from high school and becoming a nurse, she also was deeply prejudiced against Italians. I have no idea what the source of this prejudice was, whether it was derived from personal experience or from generalized xenophobia. But her animosity against Italians was such that Doris actually told Ernest and Julia that Paul was Spanish. They seem to have believed her. They certainly must have wanted to believe her because they spoke with me many years later at their surprise when they discovered Paul came from an Italian family that ran a tavern in Little Falls on Route 46. I mention this detail for an important reason.

Doris contended that her marriage was at first difficult, then a failure in large measure because Julia was so antagonistic toward Paul's Italian heritage. He knew very well that he was not liked in the Jacobus household, so he either stayed away or cut his visits short. He did not want to be the victim of barbs or complaints, so he did the easy thing: he disappeared. When he did drive Doris over to see our family, Paul was so angry that Doris says the drives home were themselves hair-raising anxiety trips. She did not yet drive herself at that time, so she was completely dependent on Paul.

He was not a successful husband. I thought he was a nice guy as I grew up and he found it easier to talk with me than anyone else in the family. He never talked about anything important beyond a few conversations we had regarding subjects that mutually interested us. He was in the music business for a long time, servicing juke boxes in his area of New Jersey. He maintained them, changed their selections, collected the money, and generally felt himself in the heart of the entertainment business. For that reason he was able to advise me about hi fi equipment when I came of age. But earlier than that he sometimes gave me a ride in his car, a wonderful pre-war Lincoln Zephyr. He wrecked it one day going through an intersection when a spider lowered itself from the rear view mirror and caused him to lose control of the vehicle while trying to deflect the spider from his face.

After the war, Cullen came back to 7 Webster Place. I was about eleven years old when the doorbell rang and a man in uniform came to the door and asked for my mother. I did not recognize him. But I had studied the various chevrons that army men wore, so I knew he was a technical sergeant and called to my mother, "Mom, there's a technical sergeant here to see you." I had forgotten Cullen entirely by that time and during this visit, I did not stay near my mother and listen in on the conversation. I heard only later that he had been devastated by the fact that Doris had married someone else. He had his heart set on their being married as soon as she was out of high school and it was terribly difficult for him to deal with his feelings. One thing he did tell Julia was that if Doris ever left her husband he would be there for her. He would marry her in a minute. My mother knew he meant it and she eventually told Doris about the meeting and about his feelings. Doris at that time was a mother and was not entirely happy with her married life. But she felt trapped and could do nothing. Cullen married one of my mother's cousins only a few years later.

Every so often Doris would come to visit at 7 Webster Place. She never feel very much at home there, so her visits were limited and not always successful. She once brought both her sons, Paul Jr. and Kenneth, on a visit but they, too, felt criticized by Julia and as a result did not feel very close to their grandmother. Although they lived only twenty minutes away throughout their lives, neither Paul nor Kenneth ever visited their grandmother on their own, not once. Even more remarkable, neither Paul Jr. nor Kenneth ever introduced their grandchildren to their grandmother. So my mother had great-grandchildren whom she never met even though she lived only a short distance away. I have no idea if this was a form of punishment or simply a matter of indifference. It could have been both.

At first, for a short time, Doris and Paul lived on their own in a new garden apartment in Paterson and those years seem to have been happy. We visited her there after her first child was born and the household seemed cheerful and pleasant. But after a short time they moved to an old barren house next to Paul's father's tavern. It was a small, run-down house on a major, noisy highway. It was laden with the dust from the road and there was no lawn, no flowers, no landscaping. It was simply barren. Doris was left there most of the time with the children and could not have been very happy. She told me that Paul ordinarily left her a dollar, four quarters, for the day's expenses. Paul's father, Gregory, was a crude, boisterous, and sometimes brutal man with no shred of manners, thoughtfulness, or charm. He treated Doris with respect, but was often mean to Paul and his children. When Gregory died a multi-millionaire, he left nothing to his son Paul.

Doris tried running a hot dog stand in front of her house. It was a busy highway and cars careened around the corner near her in such numbers that it was clear she could count on plenty of business. She served hamburgers, hot dogs, coffee, and milk shakes. And she worked very hard in the business even though she had two sons to raise. Her husband was off and away at his job during the day and in somewhat later years he became an adjunct police officer in Paterson and spent some of the evenings in patrol cars. When we visited he was invariably out "with the police." Unhappily, though, some of the time he was with other women. Eventually he got one of them pregnant, ending his marriage and leaving Doris tired, disillusioned, and deeply hurt. She had done everything she could to get along in Paul's family, but nothing was enough. She was expected to do everything, raise the boys, keep the hot dog stand running, manage the house, and all without a car of her own or a means of getting away even for a few hours from a situation that must have been intolerable.

Doris's early life as a high school drop-out had long lasting consequences. Her home on Route 45 had no books, no place for her children to study. Instead it had a large television set that was on almost all day. This was at a time when we had no television in our own home. Doris's children seem to have had special reading problems that went unrecognized, and as a result of various forms of neglect, they also became high school dropouts. Both of them grew to have children of their own, and those children are also high school dropouts. The next generation, although already producing some dropouts, may some day break that cycle. But the painful thing is that it is a cycle and because it produces limited economic opportunities it is almost impossible to break.

Doris clearly had many regrets. In later years she talked about Cullen and even asked me to search out his cousin on the internet, but when I did so, she did not call him. I think that she must have fantasized that her life would have been very different and much better if she had waited for Cullen. However, Cullen died in the early 1990s, and if they had been married things might not have been as romantic as the promise of their adolescent years suggested.

Doris in 1995

Doris was haunted by a difficult past, but after she was divorced she made the best of the present. She sold her house because she did not want to have it attract Paul if he became disillusioned with his new wife. When she found a place to rent in Paterson she worked for a neighbor who ran a small upholstery company. The odds were against her, but with help from my father she began to take courses at the local community college, ending with a nursing degree that permitted her to work in a hospital. By determination and with a resurgence of the ambition that had moved her to want to go into nursing before she married, she transferred to a four-year program, got her degree and took a job working a regular schedule as a nurse in a nursing home run by the Little Sisters of the Poor. She found that helping others kept her sane and gave her a sense that she was doing something worthwhile with her life. Hers was the familiar pattern of the survivor.

My sweet, beautiful sister died suddenly in1999. She suffered an aneurysm in the brain while at work. She died in a few days without regaining consciousness. The priests gave her a remarkable funeral and wake in the Catholic nursing home where she had worked most of her later life. Because Doris was part of the nursing home "family," the services were elaborate, magnificent in many ways, and visually beautiful. Our four year old granddaughter, Caitlin, sat in the evening looking at Doris's open casket, with flowers and candles in the sepulchral light, and said to her mother, "When I die, I want it to be just like this."

White Flight

From my birth in 1935 to 1952, when my parents reluctantly decided to move away from 7 Webster Place, our street was an interesting amalgam. Most of the buildings were turn of the century wood frame single family houses. Two of my best childhood friends lived in the only apartment house, halfway down the street. It was set back and had a cement semi-circular drive for letting off and picking up residents. The apartment house had a special cachet for us. We thought that its residents were better off than our family because they had more luxuries than we did. For example, virtually all the people in the apartment building drove post-war cars in 1948 while we still drove our 1931 Model A. Some of the residents owned shops and stores in the neighborhood and my own friends who lived there always seemed to have more pocket money than I did.

Our house was built around 1915 as a wedding present for a daughter of the Benedicts, whose mansion was around the corner on the swankier South Harrison Street. The huge and stately Benedict mansion, empty except for a caretaker, lay directly behind our house. It sat on at least three acres of land, very unusual for that neighborhood. Much later I realized that the house must have been owned by heirs who had long since abandoned our neighborhood and were waiting to get the right price for the property. In 1951 they sold it to an insurance company for whom my mother would work as a secretary in the 1960s.

Webster Place was half in East Orange and half in Orange. The people who lived on Webster Place, not more than a thousand yards long, were almost all white in East Orange, where we lived.

The people in the other half were all Black. The dividing line was absolute but invisible: a town line. The Black half of the street was in a completely different town. The apartment house, whose tenants were all white when I lived there, was the last building on the East Orange half of the street. The houses on the Black half of the street were the same size and quality as those on the white half. Any stranger to the community would not have noticed any difference between the homes in either town. They were all well-maintained one or two-story houses set back from the street with neat lawns and driveways. The difference was that we rarely socialized with our neighbors in Orange. But it was also true that we socialized very little with our neighbors in East Orange, except for the boys my own age who lived across the street.

Color seemed to absolutely separate us, despite the fact that people who lived on the Black half of the street would often walk down past our house from Harrison Street. They would walk up (there was a very slight hill up from Orange) to the shops on Harrison Street and return with their shopping bags. We knew a few of our Black neighbors by sight and would often say hello to them from the porch in the summer. They would respond kindly although they did not know our names, nor did my parents know theirs. This was not entirely strange because we were familiar with only a few of our neighbors in East Orange. People kept much to themselves at that time.

Webster Place "began" at Harrison Street and "ended" at Oakwood Avenue. Oakwood Avenue was somewhat run down although it could not be considered a slum. There were a few general stores on that avenue, a small church, and a big lumber yard. There was also a large YMCA that once suffered a gas main explosion. The front of the building was blown off and the rooms were exposed, their floors leaning down weirdly. It was very much like the pictures we see today of bombed embassies and other buildings. People were injured, but I do not remember that anyone died. Nevertheless, it was a colossal event in the neighborhood.

I never felt comfortable on Oakwood Avenue. I always felt threatened because I was white. No one ever did anything explicit to me to make me feel I was in harm's way. People sometimes looked at me oddly as the only white boy in the area--as I sometimes was--but no one ever went out of their way to make me feel as if I were in danger. It was simply the perception that I started with as a child and never quite outgrew while I lived in East Orange. I sometimes saw young Black people--older than I, but still school age--walk up from Oakwood Avenue past me as I played near my house. Usually we said nothing, but there were one or two kids who would be kind and greet me cheerfully. We had a "hello" relationship. At that time I remember being curious and wanting to get to know them better.

Oakwood Avenue also had an elementary school which was all Black except for one boy, Frankie Elia, who was my playmate when we lived at 22 Webster Place. He lived on another street, in Orange, so he went to the Oakwood School in Orange. I do not remember his ever complaining about the school nor did he ever talk about it. He just went there and seemed to be fine. There was a time when my parents thought I would have to go to the Oakwood School. I remember not being comfortable with that possibility, partly because I had a few friends who went to Nassau School and partly because I would be only the second white student. Apparently the school boards of Orange and East Orange conferred and offered my parents the choice because I lived so close to the Oakwood School. However, our house was in East Orange, so I went to Nassau School, which was a full mile away.

When I was five and six years old I used to get up in the morning and be out on the street before the other kids went off to school. Mrs. Osborne, from a nearby street, drove children from our street to Nassau School for $1.50 a week, quite a bit of money then, paying off her new cars in that fashion. I used to watch the kids pile into that car with a great sense of envy. I wanted to go to school so badly I would cry when the children left. My mother kept me home as long as she could and as a result I never went to kindergarten. I began school in first grade. I finally got my chance to drive in the car that took the whole neighborhood to school. In those days we got out to go home for lunch, which I often did in the later grades, walking one mile to get home, eating very quickly, then waking one mile back to school. At a certain point, when I biked to school, I took my lunch and made only one round trip a day.

My parents were suspicious of Blacks, but not antagonistic toward them. For example, after World War II, when we lived in 7 Webster Place, our old house, number 22 Webster Place, across the street, was sold to a Black man and his wife. He had been a captain in the U. S. Army during the war and walked up and down the street with a ramrod straight back. He was tall, strong looking, and handsome. My father got to know him, always referred to him as "the Captain," and sometimes talked with him about the house they had shared. My father always spoke approvingly of "the Captain," and looked forward to opportunities to talk with him. "The Captain," however, was very taciturn and made his conversations brief and to the point. He always greeted me kindly, as I did him.

There were riots on Oakwood Avenue some time when I was very young. Houses and businesses were burned on Oakwood Avenue, but the damages were entirely concentrated down on the avenue. No damage was done to any building on Webster Place, whether in the Black or white neighborhood. We drove slowly down Oakwood Avenue one day after the rioting had stopped and the fires had been put out. It was painful to see. Parrow Street, off Oakwood Avenue, just below where Webster Place ended, was especially poor looking. It had many ancient wooden tenements which, for me, defined what a poor neighborhood was. We went there only rarely, and I know that I always felt threatened when we drove through and I could not feel comfortable looking at the people who sat on steps or stood by doorways on Oakwood Avenue. For reasons I understood later, they were not friendly toward us and stared back at us with what seemed like expressions of anger or resentment.

I was around twelve when I began to develop some

friends in the Black community on Oakwood Avenue. Next to the YMCA there was a grassy playing yard that was almost the size of a football field. It was there that I had one of my most interesting youthful experiences. Benny Fletcher and I went to the YMCA one day after school to play sandlot tackle football with the Black guys who got together there regularly. We did not know any of them, and most of them didn't bother to introduce themselves. But the general leader was a fairly big kid named Percy. When we got there they were about to choose up teams. Percy decided we could play, but that we couldn't play on the same team. So they chose sides and made sure we were each on a different team.

The most remarkable thing about this experience is that Benny and I were mediocre players, but with these guys we played way over our heads. I remember the exhilaration of being counted on to carry the ball in these games. The guys from Oakwood Avenue sometimes depended on me to get the ball over the line. They blocked for me, passed to me, handed off to me. Once, when I was coming through the line on an off-tackle play I was mauled by a strange fellow called Bubbles. Bubbles was a light-skinned boy with darker patches of melanin, like large freckles. He was almost bald, and he had just moved up from North Carolina. Beating up on a white boy was not done in North Carolina, but it was acceptable here in New Jersey, and I took quite a beating from him after he tackled me and got me to the ground. Percy, whose voice was already a basso profundo, reached in and pulled him off me and said, "You pastel motherfucker, get your ass over there and cut that shit out." Bubbles, in turn, called Percy a "purple-ass motherfucker," and I got my first lesson in the gradations of Black on Black anger.

But what moved me was that Percy stood up for me and made sure that kind of thing did not happen again.

We had some fights. That was common enough. But when we played football on Oakwood Avenue the only person I was permitted to fight was Benny Fletcher, and because he was a pain in the ass much of the time we often wound up in the middle of a group of our football buddies, fighting it out in the autumn gloom until one of us called out enough. Out of this experience I realized that the Black guys I played with were a lot like the white guys I played with. In later years, when I played ball in a predominantly white situation, we treated the only Black players with great respect. We made sure they didn't take any crap from any of the guys, and we treated them as if they were the stars of the team. The very same thing happened to Benny Fletcher and me when we were in a predominantly Black situation.

My growing up on Webster Place made me understand at least some of the similarities between white and Black people, and while I early on had unreasonable fears of Black people, I outgrew them and can thank my neighborhood experience for giving me a real understanding of my neighbors. One day in the early 1960s we had a Black friend, Al Slocum, in New Milford, who had grown up in East Orange around 11th Street. When we first met and talked we soon found out that we had neighborhoods and experiences in common and he relaxed immediately. He told me, "Man, when you see me coming down the street you see a man coming down the street, not just a Black man coming down the street." At the time I wasn't sure he was right, but the more I have thought about it over the years the more I understand what he was saying. Because of my experiences growing up, Black people were no more a novelty to me than white people were to him.

The war produced many kinds of shortages for both Blacks and whites. One of my chief activities was taking part in paper drives. This gave me the chance to get to see the insides of some of our neighbors' houses, since they all saved newspaper and other paper goods and I hauled the papers in my wagon to the recycling center near Brick Church Station. I used to make trip after trip from some of the houses, moving huge stacks of papers that had to be steadied as I negotiated the ice-heaved bluestone sidewalks.

Because of shortages, certain foods and supplies could not be obtained except rarely. My father's best friend, Larry McManus, was a cheerful fellow about my father's age, and a pal of his before he got married. Larry was a bachelor living with his sister and he was a cheerful fellow who knew how to have a good time. He was also a manager of a grocery and on one occasion he got my father a fantastic deal: a huge carton of toilet paper that lasted the family about two and a half years, the worst period through the war. We had the carton in the basement of 7 Webster Place and it was my job to go down and replenish supplies. It was also my job to go to the A & P with my father on Saturday when he did the food shopping. My mother never went food shopping for as long as I can remember. My job was to watch our shopping cart and make sure that no one took out the foodstuffs that required a rationing coupon. The fact is that people really did take things out of other people's carts when they could. I stopped several people when I was eight and nine years old and they did not take my challenge lightly.

At that time the kids I played with were always on the alert for spies and saboteurs. On our side of the street, near the apartment building was a large black house set far back from the street. The man who lived in that house was Japanese and we held him in suspicion of espionage. We would see him walking up and down Webster Place regularly, fairly tall, about sixty years old, slightly hunched over. He would rarely speak. Eventually I began to say hello to him and he responded with a kind hello. One day my friend, Marvin Fine, who lived in the apartment house, and I talked with him and the Japanese neighbor invited us into his house. We went and he showed us what he was working on. He was a stage designer and had astonishing working models of various sets that he had built. I remember looking at them and wondering what to make of them. I knew nothing about stages or stage design and I thought this a very exotic activity. Before we left, we asked him what the word "Banzai!" meant, since we heard every Japanese soldier in all the war films shouting that word when they attacked. He explained that it was equivalent for "Hooray!" As far as I know, this man was not interned, nor was he harassed by police. I have the feeling now that he may have been a distinguished theater person.

Webster Place in the 1940s enjoyed a few old-fashioned institutions. The tradition of the lamplighter was still intact up until we left East Orange. The lamplighter would begin walking down our street from Harrison Street each evening at dusk and pause to light the gas lamps on both sides of the street. The illumination was soft, steady, and incomplete. I do not recall anyone thinking of it as romantic, and some people may have thought of it as dangerous. One night a woman screamed terribly up near Harrison Street near the second gas lamp and, when neighbors responded by coming from their houses to help her, an assailant, a large man, ran up toward the avenue and got away. She had been hurt and fell to the ground sobbing and may have been robbed. I know we were more worried about whether she had been hurt than whether she had been mugged. Webster Place was not especially dangerous, but people were nonetheless cautious and on the alert.

Another old fashioned institution was the milkman and his horse-drawn cart. He came regularly from Alderney's Dairy or Beck's Dairy and delivered fresh milk in glass bottles. They were placed early in the morning on our back doorstep and in the winter the cream would freeze on the top and push up the waxen bottle cap. For some reason I hated cream when I was young and would immediately shake the milk as soon as we got it inside. Sometimes my mother would pour the cream off into a pitcher, but I do not recall that she liked it very much herself. Homogenized milk came to our house only in the 1950s and it seemed like a blessing at the time.

The coal man was a regular visitor in the winter and in the late fall, before the snow began. He would back his coal truck into our driveway and I would open the cellar window over the coal bin where he would place a metal chute that led from his truck to the window. The coal was dampened by a hose before he started so that the coal dust would not rise up and travel through the house. There was a time, before the metal chutes became popular, when the coal man would fill a large metal-framed canvas basket and carry the ton of coal load by load and dump it through the window. It was an event when the coal man came.

The ice man had his appointed rounds as well. We had an ice box for as long as there were ice boxes on Webster Place. We could never keep meat in the ice box for more than a day, which explains my mother's distaste for beef and hamburgers. Whatever flesh we ate had to have been bought and cooked on the same day. Of all these old style accommodations, the only source of excitement came from the milkman, whose horse would, despite its iron hobble, suddenly take off down the street at a gallop, risking injury and catastrophe.

Automobiles were a staple item on Webster Place. All day long and all night long, both sides of the street would be lined with parked cars. We played football, stoop ball, baseball, and other games out in the middle of the street until dusk every day. We ran interference with the parked cars and even dared the cars moving through the tightly constricted spaces. I often caught a football while throwing myself on the hood of a parked car, and more than once I ran into a sturdy bumper while running one play or another. We often took solid bruises from the cars and never thought much of it.

What I did not know when I was a child in school is that East Orange had been going through a profound social change for some time and that it would undergo an even more profound change in the immediate future. For some reason I still remember one of the older fourth grade teachers at Nassau School telling us that not many years earlier students were brought to school in horse drawn coaches by their parents or by their servants. This was an exotic idea at the time and it stayed with me only because it was so strange. Now I realize that what she was telling us is that the students coming to school near the turn of the century were often from very privileged families because the community itself was then much more wealthy than it was while we lived in it. A close look at some of the early housing stock could have told me the same thing if I had understood how to appraise it.

At Nassau School my class had a mix of Catholics, Protestants, Jews, but only one Black student, Mackie, Richard Macklin, who was our star athlete and, while quiet and withdrawing at times, a good friend. His younger brother was in the class below ours and he, too, was friends with everyone. Despite the fact that I lived on the edge of town and next to one of the largest local Black neighborhoods, it was not entirely clear to me as a child that neighborhoods had special distinctions between income or race. Ours was not a wealthy area except for the real estate on Harrison Street, with its huge apartment houses and an occasional mansion dating from the late nineteenth century.

Behind our house, for example, and facing on Harrison Street, was the Benedict Mansion, a large nineteenth-century French design with stucco exterior walls. It approximated a delicate country chateau. The interior was completely furnished with colorful wall paper, bright upholstery, and exceptionally well lighted rooms with oversized windows. I visited the upstairs once and found the rooms with most of the furniture intact and most of the spaces palatial, especially in comparison with our own home. Obviously, this was one of the mansions from which students, complete with their horse-and-carriage house on the property, once emerged to attend Nassau School.

But that was long ago. All the years I lived in East Orange, the only people who lived in the Benedict house were simple caretakers, the Schlachters. They were not among the brightest people we knew in those years. The son was constantly being held back in school and became essentially a bully among younger kids. He bullied me for a while until I got away from him. His parents were crude and close to illiterate, which I discovered as a young boy sitting on their back porch when I helped the bully's mother read a comic book. I was shocked to discover how limited a vocabulary she had.

In a sense, I got to know much more about East Orange when I went to East Orange High School. What surprised me was to find that the student population was more than one third Black. The sections of East Orange nearest to Newark had a much greater African-American population than the neighborhoods closer to Orange. One oddity in East Orange High School was that its indoor swimming pool was always empty and always closed. It is possible that the Polio scare closed it, but it is much more likely that white parents did not want their children to share the pool with Black students. I was told that by older students in high school, but it seemed unreasonable to me at the time. Now I think it is probably the true explanation.

East Orange High school had a couple of thousand students and the quality of instruction I received was excellent. The teachers were demanding and the workload reasonably high. I was in a college preparatory track whose classes did not have one-third Black students. That most Black students were in the business track did not seem unusual to me when I was fourteen. Most of the time we were all together in the school in a number of ways, between classes, in gym classes, in extra-curricular activities, and many other ways. I sang in choir and for a while sang with the gospel choir, which was ninety-five per cent Black. I spent many hours in the baritone section and made good friends. They often told me stories about their home life and I sometimes found their stories at odds with the way things worked in my home, but again, I was young, uncritical, and simply curious. Their families were often as large as mine was, but they had more stories of adventures and close calls. On the whole, however, I found myself accepted among my Black school friends, and most of the time very much at ease. There was not all that much difference between us.

However, there was one difference, and partly of temperament. When I was a child in East Orange the level of violence was very high among young people. I remember telling my parents that they lived in a very different world in East Orange than I did. There were gangs of mainly Italian kids in my neighborhood who wielded considerable influence through threats of violence. They were not like gangs today. They did not conduct local criminal activities, although they sometimes stole cars and got away with their doings. It was more of a sense of protecting turf. These gangs were not involved in any racial violence at that time. But they were often a threat to me and I was fortunate not to be in their way.

I did not see or notice any Black gangs at that time. But I was aware of incendiary actions among Black students. More than once I saw ferocious fights among girls in front of the school, with screaming, hair pulling, and a mob around them urging them on. I did not know any of the fighters personally. My friends in the choir and my friends in gym were not involved. However, the most frightening thing I saw happened one warm afternoon on my way back from a soda shop after lunch, walking uphill back to school. I saw a huge wave of Black guys, most with their shirt off, possibly a hundred or a hundred fifty students all rushing and yelling and coming right toward me. I froze thinking they were after me for some reason that I could not imagine, and at the last minute they swerved to one side and another group of Black students, also yelling, and some with weapons, engaged the first group in a terrifying fight that ultimately ended with the police dispersing them all. That image has stayed with me and took on a special life when I read Dante's similar scene in *The Inferno*.

Again, I was not used to violence beyond the fist fight in the school yard, or the one-on-one brawl that sometimes erupted throughout the grades. But the high school introduced another kind of violence in the gang-up on individuals. While I was a student in high school there were several instances of Black on white violence. The white captain of the football team had been made the head of the detention class after school. I was there for some minor infraction when a Black student named Smitty committed another infraction while in detention. The captain of the football team made him sit down and reported him to the teacher ultimately in charge. The next day Smitty and four of his buddies got the football captain after school and beat him so badly that he was in hospital for the better part of a month. I still don't understand this kind of behavior, but it made a statement at the time.

What was happening in East Orange was a phenomenon that was the leading edge of white flight to the suburbs. Block Busting was an informal term that came into wide use during the time I was in high school. It referred to a procedure used by real estate agents anxious to sell as many houses as possible and anxious to make outsized profits. The technique involved frightening a white property owner with the loss of property value unless he were to sell his house quickly and almost always below current values. Sometimes using underhanded methods, the trick was to have the house bought by a Black family. Once there was a Black family on the block it was then not very difficult to threaten other white house owners with the potential loss of the value of their homes. In this way a great many white people in East Orange were persuaded to sell and leave, sometimes having serious losses depending on how long they held out.

All this worked in part because the real estate market was racist to start with. For a time segregated communities were tolerated by law, but after World War I those racist laws were thrown over. They were replaced by tacit agreements among real estate people and banks and local communities, all of which benefitted whites and kept Blacks in overcrowded communities like the Oakwood Avenue neighborhood in Orange near where we lived. As a child, I was unaware of these circumstances. My parents may have known more about these quiet arrangements than I did, but I never heard them talk about what they knew. We assumed the difference that racially bisected our own short street was caused by differences between the town of Orange and the city of East Orange.

We left Webster Place in 1952 because the racial mix of the neighborhood was changing and the practice of block busting reached us. Our house was the only thing my parents owned and in it was the only "wealth" they would ever have. Real estate agents approached my father more than once claiming that the entire block was "going Black and your house will be worth nothing if you don't sell now." It was a panicky time for many white home owners. My father knew what was happening, but he also knew that the house would sell for much

Our tiny house in Millburn

less if he did not try to sell soon. As it was, my mother did not want to move because she loved the house.

My father sold 7 Webster Place to a Mr. Jones, a Black man and his family. Mr. Jones worked at the Post Office and was a remarkable man in many ways. My family never got to know him well, and there was no special warmth between the families. It was a business deal. But my high school friend

Marvin Fine told me shortly after that he got to know Mr. Jones well and that Mr. Jones was a serious collector of jazz records and shared many of them with Marvin.

The unfortunate thing about the sale of the house is that Mr. Jones did not have enough money to buy it, and at the closing he explained that he needed a three thousand dollar second mortgage from my father. It came as a total shock to my father, but he had no choice. At that time Black people had a very difficult time getting a mortgage and banks would not always grant enough money, even to a postal worker like Mr. Jones. My father had to agree to the second mortgage, but it meant a downward spiral for my family because our next house, on Washington Street in East Orange, became much more expensive than my father expected and he could not maintain it. We moved out of it in less than a year, again at a loss. We then moved to a small house in nearby Millburn, but that house was also too expensive to maintain and my parents sold it in less than a year. Our family ended up in West Orange in 1953, where my father died in 1987 and my mother in 1994. It was a very basic two bedroom house that was smaller than the second floor of 7 Webster Place, and my mother always hated it. Yet, its small size and its easy upkeep turned out to be a blessing to both my parents in their old age.